MANAGERIAL COURAGE

MANAGERIAL COURAGE

Revitalizing Your Company Without Sacrificing Your Job

HARVEY A. HORNSTEIN

John Wiley & Sons

NEW YORK • CHICHESTER • BRISBANE • TORONTO • SINGAPORE

Copyright © 1986 Harvey A. Hornstein
Published by John Wiley & Sons, Inc.

All rights reserved. Published simultaneously in Canada.

Reproduction or translation of any part of this work
beyond that permitted by Section 107 or 108 of the
1976 United States Copyright Act without the permission
of the copyright owner is unlawful. Requests for
permission or further information should be addressed to
the Permissions Department, John Wiley & Sons, Inc.

This publication is designed to provide accurate and
authoritative information in regard to the subject
matter covered. It is sold with the understanding that
the publisher is not engaged in rendering legal, accounting,
or other professional service. If legal advice or other
expert assistance is required, the services of a competent
professional person should be sought. *From a Declaration
of Principles jointly adopted by a Committee of the
American Bar Association and a Committee of Publishers.*

Library of Congress Cataloging in Publication Data:

Hornstein, Harvey A., 1938–
    Managerial courage.

    1. Industrial management. 2. Leadership. 3. Organizational
behavior. I. Title.

HD31.H658   1986   658.4'092   85-29553
ISBN 0-471-01052-9

Printed in the United States of America

10 9 8 7 6 5 4 3 2 1

For Madeline, always

*The spirit of venture is lost in the inertia
of a mind against change.*

ALFRED P. SLOAN
My Years with General Motors

ACKNOWLEDGMENTS

Hundreds of managers volunteered their time to tell me why organizational innovation so often depends on courageous individual initiative. Their willingness to help provided valuable information about both the psychological profiles of courageous managers and the organizational conditions which stimulate and stifle managerial courage. Because of their inputs something practical can now be said to all people in organizations about how they might behave courageously without committing career suicide. The experiences and insights that were shared by these hundreds of managers also show us how to manage people and organize work so that obstacles in the path of courageous initiative are removed, and the flow of innovative ideas is increased.

For the most part I do not know who these hundreds of managers are. Their efforts were donated anonymously, and I cannot thank them individually, by name. What I can do, however, is praise them collectively and hope that this book, which they made possible, proves worthy of their contribution.

Acknowledgments

Friends and associates, living in the United States and Japan, also deserve a warm "thank you." More than fourscore of them helped me to gather information by distributing questionnaires and arranging interviews with clients, social contacts, and coworkers. I asked them for help and they gave it. The list of names is too long to present here, but that is probably not necessary anyway. They know who they are and they now recognize how appreciative I am.

Three friends and colleagues, Gary Bridge, Chloe Z. Clark, and Suzanne Fenwick also deserve a "thank you." They were extremely helpful. Gary provided expert help on the questionnaire, and Chloe and Suzanne were always ready to work when difficult tasks needed doing (they labored to organize the data for analysis and sat for hours, struggling to get comprehensible printouts from the mainframe computer at Teachers College, Columbia University). In addition to sharing ideas, Chloe and Suzanne helped me to prepare the manuscript. They also were eagerly supportive of this project on those occasions when the end seemed hopelessly out of reach.

My daughter Jessica, who is now a teenager, was not involved with the substance of this book, but helped me to write it nevertheless. Jessica was unfailingly pleasant, and tried hard to stay interested when I talked with her, sometimes at too great a length, about what I was learning. On the other hand, Alison, my five-year-old daughter, actually provided substantive help by sharing an idea that she had: "What is that book about, Daddy?" she asked me one day. "Courage," I answered. "Do you know what that is?" "Of course," she responded indignantly, "it's what the cowardly lion in the *Wizard of Oz* wanted, but really already had. Why don't you tell people about that?"

She was right. I should remind you of the cowardly lion. Lots of people are like him, managers included. They are much more brave than they give themselves credit for being. Alison deserves thanks and commendation for the insight.

My wife, Madeline Heilman, is a coprofessional. Her research on gender and discrimination in the workplace has regularly received professional praise and mass media attention. Her excellent skills, exemplified by those successes, she offered to me at every stage of this project's development. When I first had the idea, Madeline worked with me to make it more sound, giving me hours of her time. As I sat with that wonderful wealth of information from managers that needed sifting and interpretation, she spent countless hours more. And, after a draft of the book was prepared, she read every page, thinking, commenting, and doing what she could to improve my effort. Add still more time, much more.

Graciously, she will deny that all the effort amounted to much, refusing any professional credit. But I know better. I cannot compel Madeline to take a share of whatever worth this book might have, but I can dedicate it to her, and that I have done, with ever-growing love and respect.

H.A.H.

CONTENTS

Contents

MANAGERIAL
COURAGE

Chapter One

Managerial Courage and Organization Regeneration

"Our Future Success Depends on It"

Organization regeneration requires confrontation of the present in order to open a pathway into the future. It requires questioning the value of established organizational practice. Someone must stand up and say, "The way things are in this organization is not the way they must be; alternatives exist." Someone must challenge what is with a dream of what might be.

But such confrontation is not easy. Organizations always harbor powerful forces which discourage employees from questioning the value of established practice. By carefully dispensing perks and promotions, and by using a host of other organizational blackjacks, these forces easily find persuasive means of communicating that individual self-interest is better served by silently assenting to what is than by openly speaking out on behalf of what might be. Dissent requires courage. Employees risk a great deal when they publicly oppose the forces of continuity and their menacing protection of the status quo. If these forces are able to successfully stifle courageous behavior, then conditions are ripe for a bad case of organizational arteriosclerosis. Lacking a supply of fresh, invigorating blood, the organization's health falters, causing illness and even death.

Management interventions aimed at stimulating organization regeneration invite failure when they neglect the need for courageous behavior and the organizational forces which stifle it. These shortsighted efforts overlook one of the most pervasive, paradoxical human dilemmas of organization life: There is an unceasing conflict between what organization regeneration requires and what organization realities reward. Although the conflict is impossible to eradicate, it can be productively managed if managers are prepared to first understand and then change the organization conditions that stimulate and stifle individual acts of courage.

After 20 years of studying psychology, practicing as a management consultant, and writing about organization development and change, in the space of about 10 seconds, the singular importance of courage in organizations burst on me with unsettling clarity: It is an imperative on which organizational survival must ultimately depend. No organizational regeneration, no national industrial renaissance can take place without individual acts of courage.

Certainly 10 seconds is not a lot of time, but that's all that was required for the man with whom I was speaking to utter the two sentences which launched me on a three-year study of courage in organizations, involving hundreds of managers from companies the world over, but especially the United States and Japan.

The critical 10 seconds occurred while I was in the gentleman's office. It was spacious, cluttered with work, redolent with the piquant aroma of pipe tobacco, and, honestly, high enough above midtown Manhattan so that my ears were still popping from a rapid ascent to the unfamiliar altitude. My assignment was routine, and it certainly had not prepared me for what was about to occur. The company, a "*Fortune* magazine top ten," multinational, had contracted with me to do a "training needs analysis" for upper middle management personnel, particularly for the "fast-trackers." Part of the work involved interviewing some of the company's most senior executives. The man seated before me was one of those people. He spoke softly, looking directly at me. The disarming, down-home style was augmented by the "lived-in" climate of his office. I relaxed, enjoying the interview, which was really just beginning. The man was calmly answering a question that was broadly intended to stimulate his thinking about background issues as well as about the company's current circumstance and its implications for management education with the target group of upper middle managers.

With clear evidence of forethought, he quietly and logically told me how all the available business information led him to believe that a long-term crisis was imminent. (I intrude to tell you that the year was 1981, the company was in the petroleum industry, and subsequent events proved him right.) I listened, taking notes, until he said, "Beginning right now, organization success and survival will depend on challenging what we've been doing, on confronting existing organizational strategies, practices, and policy. It will require us (a gesture made it clear that he meant senior management) to make certain that these key managers act courageously, telling us what's wrong, and not cower in organizational corners, vainly hoping that necessary changes will magically occur without their involvement."

He continued but, with some professional guilt, I admit to you that my mind wandered. Notes scribbled in the margin of my note pad show that I wrote "Courage?

Why would a manager confront existing strategies, etc.? Why risk the cost?" Why indeed? My mind went back into gear, and my attention returned to the interview. Still concerned with managers having the courage to speak up, he was asking me if I knew the children's story "The Emperor's New Clothes." I did and immediately realized why he thought of that Hans Christian Andersen tale. It is about an emperor who invests substantial time and money in order to be well-dressed, devoting little effort to much else in his kingdom. One day two dishonest men arrive at court. Pretending to be weavers, they claim that they are able to create garments so fine that they are not visible to people who are either unfit for the office that they hold, or stupid. Vain and anxious to test the competence of his staff, the Emperor is duped. He supplies the weavers with money, silk, and gold thread, all of which they keep for themselves while pretending to weave the Emperor's new clothes.

When the clothes are ready the Emperor sends a succession of trusted ministers to see them. Not wanting to appear unfit for office or stupid, they all report that the new clothes are lovely. Finally, the Emperor himself goes to see the clothes which were so heartily praised by his subordinates. Although he sees nothing, he proclaims, "Oh! The cloth is beautiful . . . I am delighted with it."

On the day of a great procession the Emperor disrobes, dons his nonexistent new clothes, and marches through his kingdom, warmed only by the ooh's and ah's emitted by his subjects when they "see" his new clothes.

We are told that "Never before had any of the Emperor's clothes caused so much excitement as these." (We can well imagine how true that would be.) Then, all at once, with innocent persistence, a small child said, "But the Emperor has nothing on at all!!!" The youngster, you see, was not yet constrained by the forces which silenced the adult crowd and caused them, despite the evidence of their senses, to validate their superior's false, possibly health-threatening judgment.

What a fine example this story is of events that too often occur in organizations: Not wanting to appear unfit or stupid, people conform to the current consensus. Mistakes are made and then carried forward by sheer momentum, while almost everyone persists in the hollow pretense that all is well. Actually, most of the managers from whom I gathered data held this rather dim view of organization life. Half of them believed that fewer than 20% of the people in their organization ever acted courageously. In all honesty, when this project started, I held roughly the same point of view. Now I feel that it's not so wrong as it is misleading. First of all, so commonplace are acts of cowardice and conformity that we are prone to forget the many occasions on which the forces of organizational constraint are thwarted by bold action, quiet confrontation, and simple persuasion. Second, the plain fact is that people in organizations do act courageously. Therefore, if fostering organization courage is a good idea, then instead of bemoaning its infrequency, we should be asking about the conditions that stimulate and stifle its occurrence.

Answering this very question, in a way that can be used by the managerial community, was the reason for my research and is this book's purpose. My investigations have taught me a lot:

Organizational courage is neither a random event nor an uncontrollably idiosyncratic consequence of individual personality.

Organization arrangements, over which management has control, can either stimulate or stifle courage.

Organizational cultures which are excessively concerned with maintaining either hierarchical control or social harmony, for different reasons, are both severe suppressors of managerial courage.

The actions of managers who are successfully courageous follow a pattern that others can learn.

For at least one group of managers, courageous behavior is nearly always fatal. Should a member of this group feel a courageous impulse, perhaps he or she might be best advised to take a vow of silence until the impulse passes.

Beyond organizational walls, seemingly remote national and international crises have an astounding impact on individual acts of courage, an impact that poses an immediate threat to organization regeneration and a long-term threat to national economic success.

But now I have told you the end of my story, without completing the beginning. I was in a Manhattan office building, slowly growing accustomed to the altitude, interviewing a man who helped me to recognize something absolutely fundamental about organizations. Let me restate, a little differently, so that my story may continue: Organizations are the site of an inevitable and eternal conflict. On one side are the forces of maintenance and continuity, which strive to create and sustain an orderly, predictable succession of human exchanges. Opposing them are the forces of innovation and discontinuity, which seek to alter established practices. In this struggle, neither of the two regularly wears the "black hat." The protagonists are both seeking an organization's survival but in different ways. In everyday experience, it comes down to a conflict between those folks who dutifully work to manage established routines in order to ensure the successful functioning of their organization, and those who courageously challenge routines in order to do the very same thing.

No group of people who gather to do work is exempt from this conflict. It is the product of what I believe are fundamental human qualities. Very likely my first exposure to this idea occurred in 1956. I was a college freshman wearing button-down Oxford shirts and chino pants that were adorned with a useless, but manadatory, belt in the back, looking just like most of the other 1956 college freshmen. I joined them in reading William H. Whyte, Jr.'s important best seller *The Organization Man*. Without employing psychological jargon, Whyte described a group dynamic that finds its way into the life of every work group, once it has lived long enough to have a history. Describing the reaction to new ideas which are counter to the current consensus he says, "Unfortunately the group has a vested interest in its miseries as well as its pleasures." And he goes on to remind us how easy it is to recall instances where groups cling "to known disadvantages rather than risk the anarchies of change."

Unfortunately, business organizations do more than just passively cling to known disadvantages. In business organizations the authors of new ideas that challenge the current consensus are often soundly punished. Even recent arrivals to corporate life quickly recognize that organizations provide the guardians of the current consensus with a vast arsenal of tools for punishing what they consider misbehavior. People who courageously challenge established practice can be fired, given minimal or no salary increases, passed over for promotions, burdened with assignments (especially unpleasant ones), stigmatized with poor performance evaluations, ostracized by powerful in-groups, and excluded from those critical, albeit informal, information networks that exist in every company. And, make no mistake, the arsenal is not exclusively for use by one's bosses. Subordinates have their own means of protecting the current consensus. They can ruin reputations, sabotage their superior's performance, and create enough commotion so that their superior's bosses conclude that he or she is "unable to manage people."

Everyone knows war stories where either bosses or

subordinates used such weapons to punish an individual's courageous attempt to change established organizational practice. I like war stories, and this book has a healthy sprinkling of them but, truly, by themselves, war stories are unsatisfying to me. I was originally trained in experimental social psychology, a research discipline. It is a training that exposes one to scientific method as if it were an object of religious worship. War stories just don't carry much weight after that kind of educational experience. They are illustrative, intriguing, and may even contain a kernel of truth, but as the Yiddish expression goes, "For instance is not proof." I wanted more systematic information about how organizations attempt to suppress courage. What devices are used? When?

Are courageous acts punished even when the idea is proven right? How does an organization's treatment of courageous members affect the courage of others? Responses to these and other questions revealed some unexpected answers: You **can** buck the system and get away with it. Surprisingly, you can even buck the system and get away with it when your idea is a loser! Who you are, the composition of your supporters and your opposition, the issue that you challenge and, especially, the way that you challenge the system affect the organization's response to your courageous act. In fact, I am pleased to report that although the forces of continuity have a powerful arsenal at their disposal, they are hardly indomitable.

Claims like this can be misleading, and I feel compelled to make my position clear. None of what has been said should be interpreted as a wholesale condemnation, by me, of either the forces of continuity or the conventional behavior that they produce. On the contrary, one consequence of my investigation of managerial courage is that I have developed a healthy respect for conventional behavior in organizations. After analyzing data from hundreds of questionnaires and dozens of interviews, it is clear to me that while courageous behavior is essential to organizational progress, conventional behavior is essential to smooth day-to-day organizational functioning. Ultimately, organizational success rests on management's ability to strike a productive balance by managing both the forces of continuity *and* discontinuity.

Even before I walked out of that office, the excitement of my new insights was disrupted. I felt uneasy, disturbed. I knew that this executive's concern about his organization's capacity for regeneration was not an isolated case. The 1970s was economically disastrous; its unhappy legacy for the 1980s is a desperate need to revitalize business organizations. When I questioned myself about whether a productive balance was being struck between the forces of continuity and discontinuity so that the need might be satisfied, my answer was unsettling. Intuitively, I apprehended that events were accidentally conspiring to produce an imbalance. It seemed to me that despite the cries for regeneration, revitalization, renewal, and renaissance, management was actually being persuaded to engage in behavior that strengthened conformity and stifled courage.

There were warnings about the 1970s, but they went

unheeded. In 1969, Peter Drucker, that extraordinary pundit of management practice, published an article in the November–December issue of the *Harvard Business Review*. In it he said what he had said to management groups around the world, that the American economy in the 50 years following World War I was one of "technological and entrepreneurial continuity," a time which "required adaptation rather than innovation, and ability to do better rather than *courage* to do differently" (note: italics added). But, Drucker warned, that would change in the closing decades of the twentieth century.

Drucker saw it coming. The tried and proven way of doing things dominated organizational life. I like to call it the *rule of repeated action:* In doubt? Do what you did yesterday. If it isn't working, do it twice as hard, twice as fast, and twice as carefully! For 50 years that rule worked. Then the world changed, and redoubling effort without altering direction or purpose often caused failure to occur four times more quickly.

After the fact, in 1983, Thomas J. Peters and Robert H. Waterman, Jr. lamented, "The most discouraging fact of big corporate life is the loss of what got them big in the first place: innovation." Their lament is a restatement of Drucker's warning, after we were brought to our economic knees.

America seemed defeated. Markets once dominated by American companies were captured by foreign producers. The machine tool and textile machine markets were taken by European producers, especially West Germans; and color televisions, automobiles, motorcycles, household appliances, steel, and consumer electronics were all under Japanese dominance. American management was slow in adapting to a changed world in which critical resources were in more scarce supply, energy costs escalated, third world power became more real than fancifully ideological, and the American nation experienced a decline in its political and military hegemony. Drucker's warning became reality. An era had passed.

Some people grieved the passing; others studied it. In one analysis of the defeat, *Industrial Renaissance: Producing a competitive future for America*, three Harvard University based scholars, William Abernathy, Kim Clark, and Alan Kantrow, offer compelling evidence to illustrate how the current condition is substantially a consequence of industry's failure to adapt to a new pattern of competitive reality. This new pattern was born in social, financial, and technological change that fundamentally altered the requirements for efficient systems of production. Taking the U.S. automobile industry as a prototypical example, Abernathy and his coauthors demonstrate how trial and error, and a series of successive business decisions eventually caused the major producers to become industrial look-alikes. They were all seeking to produce essentially the same product in essentially the same ways. The industry, like so many American industries, had entered its "maturity." Abernathy and his colleagues say that mature industries are ones in which separate producers create manufacturing and marketing arrangements based on a common commitment to a particular

product design. Richard M. Cyert, president of Carnegie-Mellon University, who discussed *Industrial Renaissance* in *The New York Times,* comments:

> In a state of maturity, only modest innovations, that
> do not require major changes in the production pro-
> cess, tend to be tolerated. Thus, a mature industry can
> begin to lose touch with the wants and needs of its
> market, and conducts its business more by concern for
> the smooth production process than for the use of the
> production.

For a time it worked. The product suited the market,
and the production system suited the product. The boat
was sailing smoothly, and there was no reason to allow
anyone to set it rocking. Then the world changed, consumer preferences, production costs, and technological
innovations altered forever the business assumptions on
which the existing commitments were based. The U.S.
automobile industry took a tumble, and it wasn't alone.
"Dematurity" of industry is what Abernathy, Clark,
and Kantrow prescribe as remedy. Dematurity means diversity, a wide range of product design and technology.
It means innovative change in the conception of product,
consonant with the new reality, rather than mere incremental refinement of product based on acceptance of the
old reality. Substantively I have no quarrel with their advice. It parallels Drucker's as well as Peters' and Waterman's. All of them claim that innovation and flexibility in
production processes are key to organizational success.

My concern is with the human problems of implementing the advice. People are not innovative because it's a good idea, nor can an institution legislate innovativeness. Remove the abstraction, reduce the advice to a practical reality, and what you realize is that innovative change must involve the expression of an idea, one that is somewhat or wholly inconsistent with existing practice. Inescapably, the occurrence of that human event, that individual expression, is directly regulated by two sets of social psychological forces, those of continuity and those of discontinuity, and not by engineering principle or the formation of capital, tighter money, tax cuts, or any other mechanistic, technological or economic remedy. In behavioral terms, an indispensable recuperative mechanism for regenerating organizations is the individual act of courage, a willingness to speak out, on behalf of the organization, despite potential costs. If the forces of continuity predominate, and courage is successfully stifled, then organizational regeneration must be endangered.

Abernathy, Clark, and Kantrow are not unmindful of the problem of implementation. They say at the outset of their book,

> Where the performance of the U.S. auto industry has grown sluggish with past successes, re-achieving . . . excellence is more difficult still, because its managers do not start from fresh ground but must first rid themselves of outdated assumptions, practices, and prejudice.

In making this statement, these scholars join hands with a host of behavioral scientists and management specialists who have recognized that organizational regeneration must involve changes in individual behavior in organizations. These people were not silent during the economic troubles of the 1970s. As the crisis deepened they offered their diagnoses and remedies. I walked out of that midtown Manhattan office pondering their advice and found it disturbing. Too much of it, it seemed to me, was exerting influence that worsened rather than improved the problem. What many of my colleagues were encouraging was a climate that would suppress organization members who had the "courage to do differently."

In order to communicate to you the influence that I believe my colleagues were having on management, I need to urge you to think about an earlier decade, the 1960s. It was a time of unusual social turbulence. From the vantage point of behavioral science, one of the most important and consequential aspects of that turbulence was the questioning of traditional relationships. One of the major vehicles for examining the nature of existing relationships and experimenting with new ones was *the group*. Probably a new zenith was reached in the number and variety of groups that met during that extraordinary decade. There were T-groups, therapy groups, personal growth groups, experiential groups, singles groups, couples groups, and women's groups. It was a time for black caucuses as well as for groups that confronted, supported, and changed individual behavior. Children in primary school met in groups in order to explore values; managers in industry met in groups in order to develop leadership skills; and men and women who lived next door, across the street, or almost anywhere met in groups in order to explore sexual "hangups."

Riding the crest of this group mania was the human relations movement, a bit less than two decades old at the time. In the forefront of that movement was an organization with which I had considerable contact, National Training Laboratories (NTL). With offices in Washington, D.C., and summer workshops in Bethel, Maine—an unlikely site for one of the human relations movement's meccas—NTL championed the cause of T-groups. Between 1965 and 1974, I worked with NTL as a staff member in their workshops and, for a short period during that time, I was also director of the organization's Center for Professional Development. Therefore, my experiences with the human relations movement are firsthand.

The intellectual roots of the movement and of NTL have at least two sources within psychology. First, during World War II research demonstrated that changes in individual attitudes and behavior were sometimes more easily accomplished by group influence than by other persuasive devices such as lecture, written materials, or coercive pressure. The explanation was simple and, in retrospect, seems obvious: Since many individual attitudes and behaviors are shaped by the norms and values of the group to which one belongs, changing individual attitudes and behavior can be accomplished by altering an individual's view about what the group desires.

A second influence emanating from psychology resulted from research on the effects of different forms of leadership on individual and group behavior. Influenced by the rise of fascism, investigators in the late 1930s and early 1940s experimentally compared the effects of autocratic and democratic leadership styles. Their findings were commonly interpreted as illustrating that in several respects democratic leadership was superior to autocratic. The spark that this observation produced was fanned by the antiauthoritarian winds of the 1960s, producing a fiery attack on autocratic, hierarchically oriented management styles.

Strongly influenced by these events, the managerial literature of the late 1960s and 1970s was filled with evidence and argument showing the practical organizational benefit of greater social harmony and cooperation as well as of participatory democratic leadership. But the advice being offered often went beyond the data. Managers were told, and still are told, to be invariantly facilitating, nondirective, relational, and people-oriented. Does the word "motherhood" come to mind? It is awkward to dispute such advice. Nonetheless, through the years challenges have occurred. One of the most recent and impressive, in my view, is from a psychologist at Yale University's School of Organization and Management, Professor Victor Vroom, who employed data from a number of research studies to demonstrate that neither autocratic nor participatory managerial behavior is invariably effective or ineffective. Rather, the value of any managerial behavior is contingent on the character of the organizational situation in which the behavior occurs.

For many human relations enthusiasts the idea that an autocratic managerial style can, at times, be as effective as or more effective than a participatory one is offensive. Their singular commitment is to a select body of data and values that argue against the real and imagined excesses of hierarchically oriented authority, which they believe are alienating the workforce and stifling individual contributions to organization success. My quarrel is neither with the data nor the values, but with the unreasonable and exaggerated claim that the data argue for the universal, invariable benefit of one managerial style. Such an unqualified claim is not only inconsistent with the totality of existing research and the evidence of one's senses, it also provides fuel for the fires of orthodoxy. Once baptized into the faith, advocates discourage managers from tenacious, unilateral pursuit of unpopular decisions, substituting the *rule of consensus* for the *role of individual initiative.*

Looking at the world scene, Admiral (Ret.) Hyman G. Rickover not too long ago bemoaned a similar state of affairs. He said,

> In most democracies, the leaders of fixed principle have now departed, leaving their standards to flexible pragmatists preoccupied with the discovery of "consensus," and survival through the use of the alluring but dangerous doctrine that a leader can serve a people well by reflecting them.

Although the implication of Rickover's observation, that a leader can never serve a people well by reflecting them, is incorrect, the remainder of his observations seems valid. When social consensus becomes the *only* socially acceptable process for a group, the climate is inhospitable to staunch, individual outspokenness and, in the absence of individual courage, group survival is endangered.

As early as 1956, Whyte issued warnings about the excesses that an undue emphasis on the group could produce, identifying NTL and the human relations movement as fostering conformity, discouraging individual expression, and supporting what he labeled as the "social ethic." This social ethic, clearly intended to be a counterpoint to the Protestant ethic, is composed of three beliefs: (1) the group (not the individual) is the source of creativity; (2) an individual's ultimate need is to belong, to be a group member; and (3) "belongingness" can be achieved through the application of science.

My education as a social psychologist, and my experiences with NTL and the human relations movement, convince me that neither the intellectual roots of the movement nor the values of its supporters demand individual surrender and conformity to group pressures, but it **is** the outcome that has often been nurtured. As I wondered about the impact of these events on the balance between the forces of continuity and discontinuity, I recalled how various human relations workshops were frequently places where individuals did their "own thing" in strangely similar ways; when beads were **in**, they wore beads, and when tears were **in**, they cried.

(One well-respected psychologist once labeled the emotional life in those settings as displays of "stereotyped affect.") People attending workshops didn't say, "I think
you're wrong," they said, "What you're saying makes me
feel uneasy" or "it gives me trouble." Rarely did anyone
have a better alternative for which they fought with un-
yielding vigor. Instead, they had a "thought which I feel
should be shared with the group." People who persisted
in advocating ideas contrary to what was popular and acceptable were "hung up" and "needed to get in touch
with themselves."

While the written word has the capacity to make
some of these temporally remote events seem silly, my
aim is neither to poke fun nor damn entirely. The human relations movement was properly concerned with
dysfunctional competitive and autocratic behavior in social life in general, and in organizations in particular,
but evangelistic zeal, combined with a natural process,
whereby individuals and groups try to become pure,
perhaps purer than others in their commitment to the
new norms and values, fatally transformed what began
as a legitimate criticism of relationships and leadership
into a new tyranny. Autocratic leadership was harshly
stereotyped as ineffective, ruthless, unconstrained self-
interest. Harmony and cooperation became indisputa-
bly good, without any undesirable costs, and disrupters
of that atmosphere were treated as if they were indis-
putably flawed, lacking *the* essential and redeeming insight. These ideas both reflected and stimulated a
change of climate in many organizations. It affected

managers: not wanting to firmly disagree and "rock the boat," because it was uncooperative, nonparticipatory, and—worst of all—autocratic, managers in many settings became enfeebled. They were rendered mere conduits for others' wishes, unwilling to mount a platform and disagree.

Emerging from that Manhattan office on that fateful day, I strongly suspected that the attack on the excesses of autocracy had produced another autocrat, softer in appearance, but no less tyrannical in its suppression of individual expression. I had to know. Was organizational courage sometimes stifled by organizational constraints born of an excessive zeal for social harmony and participatory leadership? And what happened to managers who failed to speak out, who censored themselves because they feared either the wrath of an autocratic boss or the tyranny of a social group? Dante wrote "the hottest places in Hell are reserved for those who, in a time of great moral crisis, maintain their neutrality." Was it true? If an individual lacked the courage to pronounce his or her convictions, did a personal hell follow?

Thus my thoughts unavoidably brought me to the latest influence on management practice, a clear, albeit sophisticated, incarnation of earlier ideas advanced by the organizational development wing of the human relations movement and adopted by "quality of work life" enthusiasts. I am speaking of Japanese management practices. This newest entry on the management scene also reflects an earnest and noble effort to offset the dysfunctional consequences of hierarchically oriented organizations. Paradoxically, however, without intending to, it may also be nourishing the new tyranny and the forces of continuity.

When the American business star was cresting in the 1950s and 1960s the world sought American management skills. When that star descended, business people and scholars sought a savior and an explanation. Japanese management practice provided both. A simple syllogistic analysis has been implicitly offered: Japanese companies are succeeding; Japanese managers behave differently from non-Japanese managers; therefore, if non-Japanese managers behave like Japanese managers, then non-Japanese companies will succeed also.

A long time has passed since I took a course in formal logic, but I remember enough to conclude that the argument is fallacious. Even if I were to set the rules of formal logic aside, my own experience on the several occasions that I worked in Japan, with Japanese managers, rings warning bells when I hear Japanese management practice offered by "experts" as **the** solution to organizational problems around the world. Let the buyer beware! Any unqualified purchase of this imported product could be as costly as an unqualified rejection of it. Japanese management practice offers benefit to organizational users, but it does not come free of charge. Heed the words of Arthur S. Golden, a writer, who speaks Japanese, studied about Japan, lived there, and worked, from 1980 to 1982, in a Japanese company that is part of the Matsushita empire. In a *New York Times* article he wrote:

· **23** ·

Simple emulation of the Japanese will not work . . . to imagine that the Japanese have done our homework for us and have created a model of a modern industrial society that is waiting to be copied would be foolish. If we want the same industrial and social success the Japanese have attained, we should figure out solutions appropriate to us.

It is time to debate the value of applying Japanese management practice in non-Japanese cultural settings. And, in so doing, it is essential to consider a related issue: What effect is the introduction of Japanese management practice having on courageous behavior in organizations?

Professor Edgar Schein of the Massachusetts Institute of Technology captured the issue very nicely in his erudite review of William Ouchi's best seller on the application of Japanese management practice in American companies, *Theory Z*. Schein worries that by using these practices, which produce intense loyalty and conformity, we may regress toward an "ideology of indoctrination which we so forcefully put aside a mere 20 years ago."

When I began my study of organizational courage, the questionnaires that were given to English-speaking managers were also rewritten in Japanese and distributed in Japan to Japanese managers. Their responses illustrate how the course and consequence of managerial courage in Japan is unique. The pattern reflects a society in which deference to authority and community are encouraged over counter-normative, individual initiative. Clearly, important cultural differences distinguish the Americans and Japanese.

In this book I explore whether either national group makes the most of its cultural predispositions by trying to mimic the other. America has been a land where old traditions are challenged, almost without reverence, and if they are found wanting, discarded. American myths are filled with examples of guts, know-how, and episodes where social convention and traditional authority had to be moved aside by an individual seeking to solve a problem.

Courageous dissent is written across the history of America. It was the essence of its birth and remains the heart of its folklore. Henry Steele Commager writes:

> Every pioneer who pulled up stakes and headed for the frontier registered . . . a vote of dissent from the past. Individualism, too, required non-conformity and paid dividends: The American way was always taking a short-cut to freedom, a short-cut to fortune, a short-cut to learning, and a short-cut to heaven.

Organization regeneration in America requires an American approach to innovation and change, one that builds on cultural predispositions by providing greater opportunity for individual acts of courage. Solutions creating excessive emphasis on hierarchy or harmony strengthen the forces of continuity, destroying one of the real bases on which American organizational success was initially founded: acts of individual courage.

Worried, elated, intrigued, bewildered, and enthusiastic, I walked away from that interview determined to learn something about individual courage in organizations. I wanted managers to tell me about themselves and their colleagues who acted courageously. I wanted to know what happened, when it happened, and with what personal and organization consequence. I wanted to ask common folk about uncommon acts.

The managers who helped me to understand about courage in organizations were common folk. They number in the thousands. I met these managers while I was consulting to organizations and when I taught in management education programs. They came from the United States, Japan, Hong Kong, Singapore, Malaysia, Philippines, Indonesia, Australia, New Zealand, South Korea, Greece, Cyprus, Turkey, the Middle East, Africa, South America and all the nations of Western Europe. Their ideas and stories influenced every page of this book and received solid support from in-depth data that I collected from 208 managers, 157 Americans and 51 Japanese. All 208 of them had more than 2800 years of organization experience. That's an average of approximately 13 years for each of the American managers, and 16 years for each of the Japanese managers.

As individuals these managers present a fairly ordinary picture. The American managers were largely male (84%), white (92%), and middle-aged (the average age being 38). Eight out of ten were married and had two children. An even greater number, nine out of ten, had a college degree, and about half of these college graduates also held advanced degrees.

This convenience sample of American managers labored in different work settings: Almost one out of four worked with processing industries; manufacturing, technology, and service industries each employed about 15% of the total group; and the utility industry employed a very few, about 5%. The managers' functional affiliations included line and operations, sales and marketing, staff and general management. Their positions in the organizational hierarchy ranged from first and second level supervisors and unit or department heads to senior managers and individual contributors (i.e., people with unique skills running their own shop).

The Japanese managers were equally diverse, although distinguished from their American counterparts in ways that predictably reflect idiosyncratic features of the two cultures. All of the Japanese managers were male. Their average age was 48, 10 years greater than that of the American managers. All of the Japanese managers were married, their households having an average of two children each.

Like the Americans, most of the Japanese had university degrees. The processing and manufacturing industries in Japan each employed about 10% of the group, while the technology and service industries each employed about twice that number. For reasons that may stimulate speculation, but certainly defy certain explanation, more than half of the Japanese managers declined to identify the industry in which they worked, their functional affiliation or their position in the hierarchy (i.e., anywhere between 50 and 100% more than the proportion of American managers who failed to provide information on these matters). The functional affiliations that were identified were like those of the American managers as were their positions in the organizational hierarchy, except for the fact that none of the Japanese were identified as individual contributors.

All of the people who completed the questionnaire were recruited in the same way: After nearly 20 years of organizational consulting, I have lots of friends who are either consultants or business people. Without disclosing any real details of the study, I simply asked some four dozen of them to distribute five or more questionnaires to managers with a minimum of five years experience in the work world. They knew that I wanted men and women, blacks and whites, young and old people. I did not want to know who received the questionnaires, so no names were requested and a plain, brown, prestamped and addressed return envelope was provided. As for the interviews, I made personal contacts to former clients and associates, recruited people at management education workshops and trapped a few strangers on long airplane journeys.

Using either questionnaires (for 133 American and 46 Japanese managers) or interviews (for 24 American and five Japanese managers), I asked all these people about courage in organizations. Without detailing the specific questions at this point, I think it will be helpful to tell you that I asked them to tell me about instances where they or others took an unpopular position and spoke out, despite potential costs, because they believed that their views were in the organization's best interests. This is what managerial courage is all about. It involves the expression of ideas that are different from the current consensus. Sometimes they are different because they urge change when the current consensus is to keep things as they were and are; at other times the ideas are different because they question, "Why change?" when the current consensus is fadishly and frantically pressing everyone to hop on the "let's make a change" bandwagon.

Courage also involves risk. I wanted the managers whom I questioned to understand clearly that I was interested only in those occasions when someone accepted ownership of his or her ideas, so that the risk for expressing them was not lost in the safety of anonymity. Fred Mackenzie, a manager with three decades of experience in employee relations and human resource management, makes an important distinction between courage and "pseudo-courage." Mackenzie said to me:

> Courage means risk. You're out on a limb because you believe that it is the right place to be for your organization. And that's true even when your own interests are helped in the process. Pseudo-courage doesn't involve risk. When a person speaks from a position of secrecy, strength or certainty there's no real risk; there's also no real courage, however virtuous the position may be.

There is another kind of pseudo-courage. People who go out on a limb all of the time, almost as reflex action, are not truly courageous. That kind of an invariant radical response does not convincingly reflect the sort of organizational concern that must be prominent for an act to be labeled "courageous." I screened my interviews and questionnaires, anxious to eliminate that kind of pseudo-courageous behavior, but it was unnecessary. Managers who are predictably contrary because they are always contrary were not part of my sample, nor were they regarded as courageous by any of the managers in the group. In my interviews particularly, it became clear that managers believed that the motives behind such behavior were self-serving.

This is not to say that managers who behave courageously never benefit from their acts. They may, and often do, but such gain does not nullify a principal criterion of courage, that it is an action on the behalf of something or someone other than oneself. For this reason, I did not exclude a manager from my analysis simply because he or she might have realized gain in the act of being courageous. Similarly, I did not exclude the acts of managers who admitted to being afraid. "Courage," said a senior executive of one of the world's largest multinationals, "is action despite fear. It is **not** being fearless." Finally, I did not exclude the act of a manager because it failed.

Courageous ideas are not always worthwhile ideas. I am not under the illusion that a foolish idea, courageously expressed, has a benefit for "bottom-line" organizational performance. Organization success requires more than daring and dissent. Skill and knowledge are essential. But when risk taking is stifled, the innovative ideas born of excellent skill and knowledge may be imprisoned inside people, never seeing the light of day. Therefore, although organization regeneration and growth certainly benefit from a timely meshing of courage, skill, and knowledge, it would be wrong to define courage in terms of the wisdom of the effort or its ultimate success. The essence of a courageous act, its importance and nobility are represented in the choice made by one human being to stand up and protest, to risk saying that things are not right.

In the closing pages of his book *Profiles in Courage,* President John F. Kennedy wrote:

> The same basic choice of courage or compliance **continually** faces us all whether we fear the anger of constituents, friends, a board of directors, or our union, whenever we stand against the flow of opinion or strongly contested issues. For without belittling the courage with which men have died, we should not forget those acts with which men . . . have lived. The courage of life is often a less dramatic spectacle than the courage of a final moment, but it is no less a magnificent mixture of triumph and tragedy. A man does what he must—in spite of personal consequences, in spite of obstacles and dangers and pressures—and that is the basis of all human morality.

At first these words seemed too extraordinary for the managers who helped me. I was wrong. In the moment of choice, these managers rejected the safe, popular alternative and decided to voice their convictions. Unravel each individual's choice, and a personal drama unfolds. It is a moment in the life of one person, a manager trying to do what he or she believes is right. It is drama involving a person's motives, actions, and outcomes, a story of individual experience—the joy of success, the fear of failure, and the frustration of thrashing uselessly against the enveloping muck of an organizational quagmire.

Taken together, the separate individual choices become a social drama in which the forces of continuity and discontinuity vie for dominance, and organization regeneration hangs in the balance. If courage is stifled, then the drama ends tragically with the organization persisting in established ways, ill-suited to the changing times. Such a tragedy is possible, perhaps even likely, but it is certainly not inevitable. As a result of my investigations, I have become optimistic, believing that management can deliberately create organizational conditions which stimulate rather than stifle courage. I also believe that individual managers can learn to act courageously, using tactics that increase the likelihood that their efforts will be successful. The path to realizing these practical benefits begins with understanding the character of courage in organizations. The 208 managers who answered my questions provided me with an opportunity to learn about courage. I do not doubt that they offered more than I was able to take. Nonetheless, what I learned I offer to you.

Chapter Two

A Personal Mission

"I Couldn't Live with Myself if I Didn't Do It"

While studying courage in organizations, I encountered four different groups of managers: first, there were the "courageous managers." Believing that organization regeneration was both possible and desirable, courageous managers tried to achieve it by changing the current consensus. If I may be permitted to borrow an idea from a famous psychoanalytic theoretician, Karen Horney, I believe that these managers are aptly characterized as **moving toward** a desired future organization.

A second group, "confronting managers" believed that organization regeneration was both possible and desirable, but they were angry and more anxious to punish someone, typically their bosses, for what was, rather than positively pursue any dream of what might be. Confronting managers **moved against** those parts of the present organization which they disliked. "Disaffected managers," the third group, **moved away** from the organization. To them, organization regeneration was neither possible nor impossible, desirable nor undesirable, it simply was irrelevant. Disaffected managers pursued a dream of psychological isolation, not organizational improvement.

The fourth and final group, "conforming managers," believed that organization regeneration was possible and desirable, but only by maintaining the status quo. They **moved with** whatever policies and procedures their organization was currently embracing.

Journey with me. I want to introduce you to the hopes, fears, and fantasies that motivated members in each of these groups. I have come to believe that although these four groups of managers differ in many ways, they pursue a common goal: theirs is a personal mission, to preserve a positive self-identity. I will begin my introductions with the courageous managers, and what follows are excerpts from interviews with two of them.

Courageous Managers

HORNSTEIN: What was it like for you to take that position on the issue?

F.N.: (A 54-year-old senior executive of a Fortune 500 company.) For me, behaving that way was self-fulfilling. I felt complete. Once I knew it was right, I went ahead—that's what made me whole, authentic.

* * * *

L.G.: (A 52-year-old area sales manager for a major textile firm—responding to the same question.) It really just seemed to happen. I mean, it didn't really seem as if I had a lot of choice. I wonder what was driving me.

HORNSTEIN: What do you think was driving you?

L.G.: (Silence.)

HORNSTEIN: What ideas do you have about what may have been driving you?

L.G.: (With a burst of energy.) Well, it seems silly to say. I'm a little embarrassed. Self-respect—I mean self-respect could not be with me if I did otherwise. At that moment, getting the job done right was the only important thing. It was the only way I could be myself. Does that make sense?

It does make sense, L.G., as does F.N.'s response. Both reflect the fundamental motivation of courageous managers: by their behavior they are attempting to preserve a positive self-identity. At the moment they act courageously, these managers are trying to maintain in their own minds a view of themselves as competent, worthwhile adults who are able to produce products which they themselves value. Contrary to some of my initial expectations, I now understand that managerial courage is less motivated by a strong sense of independence or a burning desire to be self-reliant than it is by an intense sense of identification with the immediate organization task. Managerial courage reflects a bridging of the internal, psychological boundary between self-identity and organizational performance on a given task, so that if performance is poor—for reasons imagined to be correctable—then self-identity is blemished. Here are additional responses to the questions, "How come?" "Why did you do it?" revealing the same motivational dynamics:

The reason I did it is that I felt it would be harder to live with myself if I didn't take the risks that I faced at the moment of speaking out about what we were doing.

It's what I call the "quiet of the evening" reason. I did it because I was more afraid of sitting alone in the quiet of the evening realizing that I had allowed us to do a wrong thing; that I didn't act when I could have because I knew better. It's not a question of being either mercenary or moral, you understand, it's just that on some important issues personal concern for your own welfare should be overcome by a sense of what's right for the work—otherwise it's all meaningless. It doesn't make any sense.

(This next response is from a 40-year-old head of an operating group in a financial institution who was in the midst of a courageous act when I had the good fortune to interview him.)

If I tell you "It's the right thing," is that too corny? I am just at a point when I cannot operate in an "emperor's new clothes" environment. If I fundamentally think we're doing wrong, then I've just got to do something about it. Maybe risk, even risk a lot—with a sense that I can be labeled as an inappropriate guy for the organization. If that's the case, then I am perfectly prepared to go to work someplace else. I don't want this to sound like too much martyrdom, because I don't think of it that way. It's just that I'm personally too uncomfortable to live with the game plan. It's not what it could be.

These responses are characteristic of courageous managers. They each reveal how closely self-identity is tied to the organization and its performance on the particular task. Note how the first of these three managers said he had to speak out "about what we were doing." The others were similar: "I was more afraid of sitting alone in the quiet of the evening realizing that I had allowed us to do a wrong thing"; and "If I fundamentally think we're wrong, then I've just got to do something about it." The sense of identity between self and organization, revealed by words like *we* and *us*, caused these managers to act, even on occasions when they were not directly responsible for what they perceived to be unsatisfactory organizational performance. What was at risk was their self-identity, not their reputation or career. Prior to the courageous act, their view of themselves was in danger of being compromised if, through silence, they imagined themselves to be endorsing what they saw as unnecessarily incompetent organizational performance. In that moment, for that issue, preservation of a positive self-identity required giving voice to their opposition regardless of other potential costs.

Certainly, these managers were not unmindful of other costs. You can easily see in their responses how each of them identified risks, fears, and potential losses, but you can also see how easily such matters dimmed in the light of a need to maintain a preferred self-identity. They had to act in a way which they believed was right for the issue at hand. Most important, on the one particular issue, the critical adhesive binding self-identity to organizational performance was the strong conviction that the facts, expertly interpreted by themselves, revealed what was right for the organization. It is important to understand that the issue was special in this way because it helps to explain why the same managers act courageously on some occasions but not on others. The evidence is that managers are especially likely to act courageously on occasions where the task being confronted by the organization involves an area where they pride themselves as having both essential expertise and necessary facts. Mindful of their skill and information, they form a judgment about currently relevant organizational policy and/or procedure. Once formed, a negative judgment cannot easily be denied. They cannot say, "Well, they know better than I"; "Who am I to say"; or "It's not my job" without surrendering their prideful claim to expertise, and suffering a concomitant loss of positive self-identity. Under these circumstances, such disclaimers form too blatant a denial of one's treasured competencies. Professional dignity, pride, and especially awareness of their own skill and information traps them. If they want to value themselves as authentic, competent, productive human beings, then they are compelled to speak out. Listen to their stories. The first from a man who was describing an event that occurred when he was chief executive officer (CEO) of a small company within one of the large multinationals:

> I was pushing the company to extend an agreement that we had with another company. My boss's boss was not pleased or supportive. It was a matter of hanging in there and not yielding to pressure. There was lots of emotional stress. It was a publicly recognized disagreement. I felt the pressure of confrontation with a

man who did not want extension of the agreement. I did it because I had no doubt that it was the right thing to do. I couldn't have faced myself if I'd done otherwise. I know myself. I'd have felt like a horse's ass, dreadful, stupid, and weak. **I had no doubt that it was right. It was my area. I was the man on the scene. I had the information more than anyone. It was right for employees and the company,** certainly at that time. The company had not much to lose and much to gain.

In the next interview another manager begins by describing his job at the time that he acted courageously.

Thirty-five years ago, maybe more, I was in charge of college recruiting in one area of the country [the United States]. People, higher-ups, wanted only Ivy League applicants; I systematically sent non-Ivy people to them. I was trying to break up the system. I felt that if I sent enough they would have to take some. I sent Jewish people, first generation minorities, people from small, unknown schools. The whole hierarchy was opposed—as far as I know—not just one person— like my immediate boss. They told me to cut it out. They'd just never done things differently.

I sent good people from scrambling schools, not rich ones. I developed cases carefully, believing that they couldn't deny the facts too often. But I was really supposed to be hiring from where the bosses came from. They wanted an image. That was right on the placement form. "Does he fit the [company name] image?"

I objected. Eventually it was eliminated. **I was doing the right thing. I had the facts.** It was important for the organization because we were getting inbred and the world was changing. Good schools were coming along and we needed creative, different people. I looked for other selection criteria: initiative, rounded people, not just grades.

If I had failed I would have been transferred and let go in time. As it was, people thought I was weird, but **I knew that I had the ability and responsibility to bring in the right people.** If I hadn't maintained those professional standards, then . . . well . . . **it was that professional confidence, the ability, that made me do it.**

This crucial sense of confidence in one's expert interpretation of available information was further confirmed in questionnaire responses. In the questionnaire, I asked managers to examine a number of statements describing possible motives for their courageous behavior, and for each statement to tell me first, whether it was an influence, and second, if so, how strong an influence was it. The list of statements were:

I could easily find another job.

I strongly believed that the facts were on my side.

I was young and could start again.

I was "backed into a corner."

I was aware of possible costs, but didn't care.

I was largely unaware of the possible costs.

I was protected by powerful organizational ties.

I was a unique resource that the organization could not do without.

I was independently wealthy.

Sixty-nine percent of the managers said that the ease of finding another job was an influence on their decision to act courageously, but only 31% of this group thought of it as a strong influence. Still fewer, only 37%, believed that they acted courageously because they were young and could start again, and hardly any of these people thought of their youth as a strong influence. So it continued: costs were not involved. Only 11% of the managers said that they were unaware of the costs, and of those who were aware, 80% felt it was a weak influence on their decision to act courageously.

Few managers, only 13%, believed that they were courageous because they had been cornered. Most, 75%, said that the protection afforded by powerful ties had no influence on their decision to act courageously. Being a unique organizational resource met the same fate: 80% said "Forget it, it played no role in my decision." Of the remainder, only a paltry 10% felt that the influence was strong.

What, then, are we left with? Well, when all the reckoning is completed, what emerges is that the only motive regularly identified as a strong influence on managers' decisions to act courageously was a belief that the facts were on their side. Eighty-seven percent of the managers who behaved courageously said that they did so for this reason and fully 80% of this group said that their belief in the strength of the facts was a strong influence on their decision to act courageously.

Let me summarize: For courageous managers, confidence in their expert ability and in their interpretation of the facts acted as a psychological glue binding self-identity to organizational performance. Consequently, when existing procedures and policies threatened incompetent organizational performance, it simultaneously threatened their positive self-identity. In order to preserve their identity and minimize internal, psychological costs, these managers had to express their opposition to the status quo and risk whatever external costs the organization might inflict.

Thus, the adult work identity of managers is both defended and affirmed in the act of being courageous. Valued and important parts of their lives, areas where they experience work-related expertise and competence, are prevented from becoming meaningless by virtue of their action. For this group of managers, silent acceptance of the organization's plans was a dreadful option.

H.H.: Why did you do it?

P.L. (A 31-year-old woman who headed a computing and management information group in a high-technology manufacturing firm.) Why? Because it was outrageous. We didn't have to work that way. I want to do things right because that's the right way to do things. What kind of fool would I have been to sit still on this one. It's why I was there. It was right . . . (pause) . . . for the good of the organization.

At the moment of action, even if angry and frustrated—as P.L. was—courageous managers are pragmatically concerned with benefiting the organization by exercising their competencies in a manner that challenges what is with a vision of what should be. Their focus, personal motivation, and aspiration for the organization clearly distinguish courageous managers from the second group, the confronters. These managers exhibit a sharply different psychological profile from the courageous ones and, sadly for them, have a very different probability of success.

Confronting Managers

R.F. is typical of confronting managers. While being interviewed he said to me:

> I couldn't believe he could do it. As I said it wasn't the first time, but this time it was more than foolish; it was dangerously irresponsible. I spoke to my people and we all believed that he deserved to be exposed for that kind of incompetency. It was ruining the organization.

The event that R.F. was recounting occurred only a few months before the interview. His boss, a former marketer and head of the product group to which R.F. belonged, had committed the group to a production plan with which R.F., a 32-year-old engineer, disagreed. The event weighed down on R.F.'s back with all the magnitude of the proverbial "final straw." He would tolerate no more from this man whose incompetence, he believed, was self-evident. After the discussion with his "people," his subordinates, R.F. armed himself with a list of particulars citing his boss' past errors and went to a mutual superior.

Fewer than five months had passed when I met with R.F. and he was cleaning his desk for the transfer that was "urged" on him to a job which, in his view, was less desirable than the one he occupied. "Malcolm," (the boss R.F. indicated was incompetent) R.F. complained, "is still doing the same thing." That irked and puzzled R.F. because, during the organization's normal review procedure, the production plan that his boss had endorsed was modified in a direction more to R.F.'s liking. Of course, R.F. had not challenged the plan as a business issue, nor had he recommended detailed alternative possibilities. He broadly challenged his boss' competence, seeking punishment and removal. In taking that approach, moving against a particularly disliked part of the organization, R.F. joined a group of managers whose risk-filled, courageous effort at introducing change regularly failed. I call them "confronting managers."

Failure is not the typical experience of managers who act courageously. To my way of thinking, courageous acts succeed when, in a manager's view, his or her organization responds to the courageous effort by exploring and, perhaps experimenting with the action being advocated. Success has nothing to do with how a courageous actor is treated subsequently, nor does it involve the wisdom of the idea. The major issue is the organization's response to what is being advocated: Does the idea receive a satisfactory hearing? Employing just this criterion, 65% of the courageous acts that managers reported to me succeeded, but the courageous acts of confronting managers did not succeed even once.

Who are these confronting managers? What motivates them? How do they behave?

Understanding **who** confronting managers are requires contrasting them to other managers in several different ways. First of all their age. Confronting managers are over 30 years of age. That is an important fact because age is associated with the success of a courageous managerial act. Ninety-four percent of managers who were in their twenties when they acted courageously, succeeded. Extraordinary! Compare that to the rate of success for the other age groups: Those who were in their thirties succeeded 59% of the time; those past their forties, 60%. Thus, although youth seems to be an advantage for courageous managers, those of us who have passed our thirtieth birthday have no reason to despair. We too succeed most of the time. But confronting managers in this sample never do. Before telling you why I think that this is so, I must say more about who these ill-fated people are.

Confronting managers focus their courageous act on

a particular issue, and do worse than any other managers who choose to confront that issue. My sense of justice and fair play would be uplifted if I could report to you that the likelihood of a courageous act's success was unrelated to the topic, if I could say "all that mattered was the merits of the case." Alas, that is unsurprisingly not so: Courageous acts which focused on business-related issues, such as profit plans and organization structure, succeeded nearly three times more often than they failed (exactly 73% succeeded). Still better is the rate of success for courageous acts related to subordinate behavior such as challenging disruptive but powerful cliques, or demoting activists who are malingering: All of them succeeded, 100%! By comparison, success was less likely when the focus was ethical principle. (False reporting to superiors or to public agencies are examples.) But, even here, nearly 6 out of 10, 58% to be precise, succeeded. It was only on the fourth and final issue that more courageous acts failed than succeeded. When a courageous act targeted a superior's behavior, fewer than 5 out of 10, only 47%, met with success. Under the best of conditions, acts of managerial courage on this topic did not fare well. But, for the confronting managers whom I questioned, the act was guaranteed to fail; no exceptions.

Confronting managers tend to be distinguished from others in still another way. A disproportionate number of these plus-30-year-old people who choose to take on superiors are childless, far more than one would expect by chance. Not surprisingly, if we examine the overall rate of success for courageous acts by managers without children, we find it is only 45%, much lower than the 70% success rate for those who are moms and pops. There can be no doubt that these two significantly different rates of success for managers with and without children reflect their dissimilarity in the issues that they choose to confront. The difference also probably reflects one other related fact that I must now share: Note how R.F. said, "I spoke to my people." That is typical of confronting managers. In seeking support for their courageous effort they form organizational alliances with subordinates that seem not to provide any useful support at all.

All managers rated the degree to which their immediate bosses, superiors other than immediate bosses, and subordinates supported their effort. In reflecting on the position of immediate bosses, 56% of managers with kids report that these bosses supported them, but only 30% of those without kids say that same thing. In describing the support of superiors other than immediate bosses, 39% of managers with kids say "Yes. I had their support," but only 22% of those without kids make the same claim. Given the difference in the degree to which managers with and without children were challenging superior behavior, these differences in support by higher-ups should come as no terrific surprise. What is more interesting and illuminating, however, is what happens when these two groups of managers describe the support that they had from subordinates, R.F.'s "people": 55% of managers with kids tell us that their subordinates supported their efforts. But, in a complete reversal of the pattern of support that managers claim was offered by higher-ups, an extraordinary 70% of managers without kids claim subordinate support. These confronting managers, 30-plus and often childless, typically saw themselves as joined arm-in-arm with subordinates in what proved to be a doomed alliance to take on authority.

From a questionnaire: "He [the boss] was irresponsibly transferring people without the benefit of discussion. It was lowering morale. I had several conversations with my staff. They were agreed something had to be done. I confronted him." (As it turned out, the "confronting" was done by memos.)

From an interview:

HORNSTEIN: What happened after you spoke with your subordinates?

B.H.: I sent the material that had been prepared describing Mr. Smith's behavior. I thought for sure that they [other superiors] would recognize how things were. We really wanted him out. Of course I didn't say exactly that. It was worth any risk to me. I did it alone. He had to go.

The action of confronting managers is mostly angry and passionate, aimed at unseating a superior who they believe has already harmed the organization and who remains dangerously incompetent. Removal, not redemption of this "enemy" is their goal.

Sigmund Freud's admonition that a cigar is sometimes just a cigar has always struck me as wise. For that reason, I always try to use common sense and everyday experience as a basis for explaining human behavior before turning to more exotic psychological interpretations. But when something looks remarkably like a duck, quacks like a duck, and walks like a duck, it makes sense to call it a duck.

There is no denying that organizations provide fertile ground for employees to express their unresolved conflicts with authority. Confronting managers may be doing just that. In contrast to courageous managers who focus on organization issues, confronting managers focus, *ad hominem*, on superiors and, instead of the dispassionate, workman-like style of courageous managers, these people seem angry. Punishment for what they believe are past organizational misdeeds, not remedy of present organizational problems, is the principal agenda of confronting managers.

Unlike courageous managers who seek to maintain a positive self-image by exercising their work-related competencies, confronting managers seek to maintain theirs by destroying an authority who, in their eyes, through irredeemable inadequacy, has betrayed organizational trust. Their eyes may be faulty. I do not know whether these people were confronting superiors of lesser ability. If I were to hazard a guess, then I would say that in all probability, some of their superiors probably were less than competent, but surely others were not. In fact, it does not matter. When their eyes were faulty, the distortions which occurred were motivated by a desire to boost themselves by taking a dim view of superiors' abilities. When their vision was more accurate, their concern and strategy still seemed more focused on bringing down a person in authority than on building up the organization.

The childless condition of many confronting managers may both reflect the underlying feelings which caused them to focus on people in authority rather than on organizational issues **and** be causing the intensification of these feelings. Parenthood provides one opportunity, perhaps a unique one, by which adults gain first-hand perspective of the role that one's own parents occupied. Through the experience of parenthood, polarized feelings about parents' real and imagined flaws and excesses are sometimes tempered. Some managers who are childless because they deliberately forego the opportunity of being a parent may be signaling their profound fear and loathing of the role of authority. (Please take heed! This is definitely not a claim that all childless managers experience these feelings or that these feelings are exclusive to those managers who are childless.) Additionally, other managers who lack the experience of parenthood, for whatever reasons, may simply lack one of life's opportunities to identify with parents. Thus, if any strong, residual feelings of disillusionment and anger about one's parents exist, then they do so unalloyed by the softening presence of empathy. In adulthood, in organizational settings, the confronting managers join with the "other kids" and suicidedly act out these negative feelings in their doomed effort to amputate what they honestly see as a gangrenous organizational problem.

Concern about the organization, and the sense that regeneration is possible, distinguish both courageous and confronting managers from a third group of managers that I met, the people whom I had earlier described as "disaffected." These people I met only indirectly and, in candor, only infrequently. In my interviews, when describing other managers who were not at all courageous, the managers with whom I spoke occasionally told me about disaffected managers. And, on just one or two occasions, I have questionnaire responses which strike me as belonging to disaffected managers. The reed of evidence, therefore, is slender and it will bear only a brief discussion of this group of managers.

Disaffected Managers

Disaffected managers lack the vigor of ambition and the passion of aspiration.

> When I spoke with this guy about what the heck he was doing he said, "Why bother? Nothing will change. My energy is for other things, not this place. . . . Battle, battle," he said. "Do you think it does anyone any good?" Christ, he sounded 90; he was only 35 or 36.

Manacled and weighed down by feelings of helplessness and hopelessness, disaffected managers give up. But their surrender of any hope for organizational regeneration is not an entirely passive, neutral acceptance of what is. They are not so uncaring. Most often disaffected managers were described as rejecting established conditions, but unable to translate their rejection into a positive program of change. If they had a vision of what should be (and I personally have no evidence that that was so), then any effort to implement it remained stillborn because of their utter lack of any sense that organizational conditions were changeable.

"I've never done anything like this," someone wrote on one of my questionnaires. "The only thing that would happen is that someone would notice me and who needs that?" Disaffected managers do not want to join, participate, or involve themselves in any part of organization life. It is without value or meaning to them. Even more, it is disparaged as a source of frustration and a place of futility. Regeneration is not possible and neither is it clearly desirable to disaffected managers. They want out, more than they want remedy. To them courage is simply irrelevant. It requires valuing the organization and its future. That is not "their bag." Personal isolation and a conviction that organization life is meaninglessly unrelated to their self-identity are the twin themes of the disaffected.

In his wonderfully insightful book titled, *The Uncommitted: Alienated Youth in American Society,* Kenneth Keniston says of the 1960s vintage, psychological isolation, with which he is concerned, it is a "rebellion without a cause," a "rejection without a program." These same words apply to today's disaffected managers in organizations. They reject conventional organizational practices and policies, and that seems a good foundation for courageous behavior, but it isn't because the rejection is so total and the psychological isolation so complete. Again, Kenniston, speaking about some 1960s alienated young people provides insight: "Central to alienation is a deep and pervasive mistrust of any and all commitments, be they to other people, to groups, to American culture or even to the self."

Courageous managerial behavior requires commitment to the self and to one's vision of the future. The disaffected possess neither commitment nor vision. They oppose, without offering an alternative. Within the organization they move away from everything and toward nothing. Their agenda is to disregard the surrounding organizational world, not to alter it.

Exactly why some managers are stricken with this form of disaffection, I cannot say. One diagnosis, on the extreme, is that the disaffection is a pure reflection of some underlying personality characteristic which would have emerged regardless of either organizational setting or experience. I do not believe that. First of all, promotion to managerial positions would not have occurred for people who behave as the disaffected managers do. Second, the tales of disaffected managers hint at a more active, committed past. At the other extreme is a diagnosis which claims that managerial disaffection has an organizational genesis, pure and simple. The argument is that people are battered about, discouraged and punished by the forces of continuity and, in the end, they surrender. Well, in the next chapter I discuss organizational conditions which suppress courage (as well as those which stimulate it), but the pure and simple fact is that lots of people are battered, but only a few emerge disaffected. Blaming the organization is too simple an answer. Disaffection among managers seems best explained as the way that some people—characteristics yet to be precisely identified—seek psychological security in relating to the obstructive, punishing quagmire which organizations can often be. In short, managerial disaffection reflects a currently unidentifiable interaction of personality and place.

Although the process remains a mystery, the outcome is obvious and it distinguishes disaffected managers from all the other groups that I encountered: Disaffected managers are organizationally aloyal. They do not care about their organizations and have no reason to be courageous. Conforming managers, the fourth group to which I want to introduce you, care a great deal about their organizations. In fact, their organizational loyalty is near pathological proportions. But, still, they do not act courageously.

Conforming Managers

Because so much has been written about conformity in organizations—I remind you of Whyte's *The Organization Man*—and, as in the case of disaffected managers, because I met conforming managers only infrequently— I will describe them in just a few words. It will help to complete the picture of how different groups of managers relate to courageous behavior in organizations.

Observing that organizations are very much concerned with accomplishing tasks in approved ways, Drucker once suggested that their selection systems are geared toward hiring people who have the "ability to do better rather than the courage to do differently." That claim is one way of typifying conformist managers. For them, what is approved as established practice is what should be. Their vision of the future is a reflection of the organization's past.

Whyte wrote about conforming managers on the very first page of chapter one in his book when he defined the words that became part of the book's title, "Organization Man." He says, "They are not the workers, nor are they the white-collar people in the usual clerk sense of the word. These people only work for the Organization. The **ones** I am talking about **belong** to it as well. They are the ones of our middle class who have left home, spiritually as well as physically, to take the vows of organization life. . . . " Later in this same book, when Whyte describes the inner workings of "organization men," he describes characteristics that are also true of the conforming managers whom I met. They go with the tide because they loathe confrontation and love approval. One manager who said that he never acted courageous wrote me a note:

> I find this questionnaire difficult since being courageous is not a good way to solve problems. It is adver-

sarial and disruptive. Routines exist for a purpose and can usually be used to solve problems. There is no sense in creating animosity by being courageous.

If conformist managers are motivated to become part of, affiliate, be included, accepted, and loved, then courage is out of the question. Courageous behavior is disruptive. It threatens uninterrupted social warmth, acceptance, communion, and belonging, all of which the conformist manager seeks in order to maintain a positive self-image. Courageous behavior is synonymous with discontinuity. It sets people apart, disrupts, challenges, and polarizes. For conformist managers, to deliberately create such "turmoil" is unthinkable. Their organizational vows include fervent commitments to the forces of continuity. They seek to provide their companies with consistency, predictability, and stability, all necessary ingredients for organizational success. The tragic flaw in the worklife of conformist managers is their inevitable failure to recognize those occasions when established practice, the organization's past, is no longer a valid vision for the future because the assumptions on which the practice was based have changed. The blind persistence of conformist managers, despite changing organization needs, is always inappropriate and occasionally fatal.

The circumstances which create feelings of positive self-identity for the four groups of managers to whom I have introduced you are very different. Consequently each group has a distinctive relationship to individual acts of courageous behavior in organizations. Rather than launch into a tedious, narrative summary of what has been said about the four groups, let me offer you a simple chart which distinguishes the groups, one from the other, in four important ways.

Managers	Orientation to organization	Behavioral goals	Belief about regeneration	Imagined path to positive self-identity
Courageous	**Move toward** future organization	To create a productive organization	Possible and desirable by changing established conditions	By affirming one's competencies through work
Confronting	**Move against** part of present organization	To punish an impaired authority	Possible and desirable if the guilty are punished	By confronting symbols of authority
Disaffected	**Move away** from total organization	To find pleasure by isolating oneself from organization discomforts	Neither possible nor desirable	By maintaining psychological isolation
Conforming	**Move with** established organization	To maintain a productive organization	Possible and desirable by maintaining established conditions	By belonging and being liked for not being different

Disaffected and conforming managers are not easily triggered into behaving courageously. Confronting managers speak out when they encounter an "impaired" authority and courageous managers do so when organization performance threatens their adult work identity. But even when this affront occurs there are times when managers are so intimidated by the forces of continuity that they surrender, becoming cowards in their own eyes.

In Act II, Scene 2, line 32 of *Julius Caesar*, Shakespeare wrote "Cowards die many times before their deaths;/ The valiant never taste of death but once." So it is with managers that I met who told me about the times that they felt cowardly, when they remained silent in order to protect themselves from unwelcome costs despite their belief that speaking out was the right thing to do.

Silenced Managers

What follows is a composite report of "cowardly" managerial behavior, based on several episodes reported to me. Everything you read is a direct quote, but from different managers:

> I can tell you about a time when I wasn't a hero. I kept my mouth shut. It was a very important meeting. A number of us had been called in to give one of the senior people some advice. In the group I was junior, but certainly one of the most informed about the problem. No one said anything about what was really happening. I wanted one of the others to speak up, but said "if they didn't I would."

I felt physically nervous, sweating, heart beating, stomach shaking—the works—you name it.

I could have done it—said something—there were openings that would have permitted it, but I chose not to. I was most knowledgable, but I didn't want to put the others in a bad light. I felt constrained by their silence, but I really knew better, more than they.

A thousand thoughts passed through my mind: Am I doing right? Should I speak up? Maybe they'll say it? Maybe they're waiting for me to say it? Am I going to embarrass them? Is it the right time?

Baloney! I should have but didn't. It was for me to do and I was chicken.

Did I have regrets? Yes! Yes! I felt horrible, not because of the substance—it was wrong of me—it had to do with human relationships . . . integrity . . . how you deal with people . . . I felt ashamed. It's not what I expect of myself.

I backed down because I had fears about how I would be treated. "I'll look like an idiot. Gee, he really scares me; he raises hell all of the time!" All these extraneous thoughts unrelated to the basic issue stopped me. The issue was, I should have spoken up. I wasn't doing my job as well as I could have.

Managers who failed to act courageously when they believed that they should have felt awful. Most frequently they said that they felt guilty and alone. Their sense of isolation was not because others fled from them

as much as they fled from others because they felt un-
worthy, a bit soiled by their misbehavior.

"I was sobbing without tears," one manager told me.
"I needed desperately for someone to say it's ok, but I
never felt so alone. There was no one. Who could I tell?
How could I? It seemed impossible. I really wanted to be
alone."

The opportunity for a manager to behave courageously can be personally profound as well as organizationally important. Once lost, the failure to seize the
moment, to stand and be counted, to give voice and not
hide behind a cloak of silence, becomes a mocking echo
that haunts one's identity for a long time.

A poem called "Courage" by Amelia Earhart Putnam
speaks to the point:

> *Courage is the price that life*
> *exacts for granting peace.*
> *The soul that knows it not,*
> *knows no release*
> *From little things*
> *Knows not the livid loneliness of*
> *fear*
> *Nor the mountain heights where*
> *bitter joy can hear*
> *The sound of wings.*

With and without malice of forethought, organizations squelch managers who would climb to mountain
heights. Intimidated and silenced, instead of hearing the
sounds of wings, these managers are doomed to listen to

their own tearless sobbing as they cower inside organizational confines sculpted by the architects of organizational continuity. Let us turn our attention from people to place and learn how organizations stifle individual acts of managerial courage.

Chapter Three

An Organizational Dilemma

*"Business as Usual . . . These Days
It's Not Good Enough"*

Organizations spawn a tension between the forces of continuity and discontinuity which careful effort can manage, but never eliminate. As a practical matter, the healthy dose of individual conformity that the forces of continuity are capable of producing is indispensible to organizational success. It helps to smooth day-to-day functioning by standardizing behavior. On the shop floor, and in back offices and boardrooms, this "sameness" gets the "product" where it needs to go, on time, fashioned in a predictable way. At the same time, however, the atmosphere bred and then fed by this "sameness" can be deadly when (not **if**) the business environment changes.

Organization adaptability and regeneration require discontinuity in either work methods or objectives which go beyond the "business as usual" incremental variety. The commitment to continuity abhors changes of this sort which threaten disruption of familiar routine and portend ambiguous risk. Management, mindful of its accountability for managing what is, rarely anticipates suffering such costs gladly. Careers and comfort are at stake, and management decision making is typically guided by both short-term, bottom-line priorities and a very understandable dose of self-interest. Consequently, management's apprehension over the looming possibility of painful costs acts as a powerful deterrent to introducing fundamental organization change. The apprehension strengthens desire for continuity and conformity and encourages the stifling of courageous behavior, ultimately exposing the organization to other consequences, frequently more lethal than those management is so frantically seeking to avoid.

No human organization avoids the dilemma that these opposing needs for continuity and discontinuity produce, nor do any finally solve it. The best of them recognize the problem and forever strive to manage it by maintaining a productive balance between these two pillars of organization life. The rest tilt toward a natural drift in organizations, conservatively trying to maintain what is, unchanged and unchallenged, by committing the crime of "**ideacide**" and stifling expressions of managerial courage.

As real as ideacide is in organization life, don't bother to look for its meaning in any dictionary. It will not be there. If it were, then ideacide would be defined as **the murder of an idea, prematurely, before it is appropriately and adequately explored.** If ideacide occurs often enough, and at critical moments, it stifles courage and threatens organizational survival.

Two naturally occurring conditions compel organizations to forever fight an uphill battle against ideacide. The first of these has its origins in the practical, economic realities of organizational life. The second has its origins in the psychology of human groups. In practice, the two conditions intertwine, strengthening one another, encouraging ideacide.

The practical realties causing an organizational drift toward ideacide are plainly evident in the words of a regional vice-president in the international division of a U.S. manufacturing company:

Once the machinery is in place, the money invested and the people hired, there is an effort to keep what you've got because it took a lot to get it and it will take a lot to get out, including maybe a few pieces of your own skin. With this attitude . . . pressure, you really don't want **really** new ideas. What you want are minor modifications which permit **business as usual.** Sometimes, these days especially, that's just not good enough.

The fact is that change can be disruptive to and inconsistent with the sizable investments of technological, financial, and personnel resources which organizations typically make in order to support existing work practices. Indeed, in a perverse twist of reasoning, these investments themselves are frequently offered as a primary justification for continuing the established work practices that they were initially designed to support. When this happens, with substantial disregard of important changes in business conditions external to the organization, the persistent commitment to established work practices is simply a hopeless effort to maintain and manage successes of the past and what once may have been useful becomes a major cause of organization degeneration.

For an example of this self-defeating spiral of events, there is no need to look further than the American automobile industry. The authors of one recent study of that industrial group comment:

Having in the most deliberate manner possible committed themselves to standardization, managers usually believed they had no alternative to sticking with it to the bitter end. As events have shown, the end has been bitter indeed.

In explanation of the comment, the study carefully records the American automobile industry's evolution from its early "immature" state (with low volume production and unstandardized products) to its more recent "mature" state (with high volume production and different manufacturers producing, in the same way, virtually indistinguishable, standardized products). Please remember, standardization and regularity in work procedures are not receiving unqualified condemnation from me or from Professors Abernathy, Clark, and Kantrow, the authors of the study that I am reporting to you. The economies that such business practices produce make any such condemnation just plain silly. What the authors said, and they seem to have chosen their words carefully, was, "managers usually **believed** they had no alternative. . . ." Standardization and regularity in work procedures become problems because they stimulate rigidity and resistance, and unnecessarily end up being obstacles to change. Feeling and acting constrained by what is, management degenerates to the point where its early patterns of experimentation and change dwindle until all that remains is petrified routine. When this happens subordinates are implicitly and explicitly encouraged to find incremental changes, **trim** and **trappings**, that do not pose any immediate threat to either the existing work practices or the high investments that people have in their continuity.

The pattern is illustrated in one study of 50 industry breakthrough inventions which discovered that not a single one came from the industry's major firms. One likely explanation is that they were trapped in a defensive, backward-looking business posture, marshalling their forces in order to manage and maintain past successes. Additional examples come from a 1982 article in *Business Horizons*, "Obstacles to Corporate Innovation." The author, Shelby McIntyre, notes that many recent innovations come from new, small concerns, not the industry giants. For example, instant photography was developed by an upstart, Polaroid, not Eastman Kodak; PBX (computer-based switchboards) is a creation of Rolm Corporation, not ATT; microcomputers were marketed first by Intel, not IBM or Fairchild; and Federal Express introduced overnight delivery, not Emery Air Freight. Young companies, and companies in young (less mature) industries, tolerate, even seek, innovative ideas for product design, manufacturing, and marketing. They do not have enormous investments, tangible and psychological, anchoring them to continuity. Production is not fixed. Operations are flexible. There is less in the way of established work practice. From all this you might suppose that industries differ in their enthusiasm for managerial courage and in the frequency with which such behavior occurs. If that's a thought you had, score "one," you are correct.

First, the broad view: Nearly all managers, 86%, thought that more courageous behavior in organizations would be better for their organizations than less courageous behavior, and 64% exaggerate this claim by saying **much more** would be desirable. Returning to the issue of industry difference, managers in the relatively new, less mature technology industry are most extreme in their views on this matter: 83% believe that **much more** courage would improve their organization's well-being. In the services industry, 75% of managers say the same thing, followed by 69% from the manufacturing industry and the same from the processing industry. In the utility industry only one manager in six, fewer than 17%, believe that **much more** courage would be a benefit.

Turning to perceived trends in the occurrence of courageous behavior, we see the same pattern: Managers in the technology industry tend to see courageous behavior on the upswing. Managers from all other industrial groups, however, tend to see it as either declining or remaining unchanged. "Where is the beef?" you ask. To what extent did these different industrial groups commit ideacide by prematurely squashing courageous initiatives? My questions to managers assessed whether their ideas received an adequate hearing. When I finished adding all the numbers, I found the very same trend emerging once again. In the technology industry, 78% of the courageous efforts succeeded, in the sense of not being rejected prematurely. The service industry was close behind with a 75% rate of success. Thus, the two industries that I believe most people would see as least mature and most developing not only voiced a desire for courage, they were also, in practice, more accepting and experimental in their response to courageous ideas than any of the other industrial groups. The processing and manufacturing industries had success rates of only 65% and 60%, respectively, and the utility industry came in a poor fifth, with only a 33% rate of success. For these "more mature" groups, speaking comparatively, courage was less encouraged, less frequent, and less successful.

Courageous initiative, it seems, fares better in organizational settings that are less settled and more developing, ones in which existing investments make fewer demands for order and social control, where variability of response is possible because existing work practices are less standardized. When conditions are more established, however, the pressure for continuity increases and the tolerance of uncommon ideas and courageous initiative declines.

Although it is true that resources initially invested in order to support established work practices can become a perverse justification for practicing ideacide and stifling courage, the simple fact is that neither machines nor money say, "No dissent," "It's never been done," "Too much risk," or "There's no precedent." People say those things. Colleagues, peers, superiors, and subordinates act to preserve the status quo. What we must keep in mind is that, above all, productive systems house social/ psychological commitments which must be breached if discontinuous change is to occur. Alliances to preserve the status quo are not simply rooted in some niggardly motivation to avoid the expense of technological or financial rearrangement. They are founded on profound, often unrecognized psychological processes that inevitably result from living and working with other human beings in groups. These processes are the second reason that organizations must forever fight an uphill battle against ideacide. Proposals for change must confront the self-protective, conservative results of these processes and that requires courage. In the final analysis, realignment of production systems with new external realities is a social/psychological problem at least as much as, and perhaps more than, it is an economic or technical problem.

The social/psychological processes that encourage continuity, conformity, and ideacide should not be thought of as pathological or irrational. They can be extremely productive and pragmatic. Conformity to rules, written and unwritten, allows human groups to maintain cohesion and sustain organized endeavor. It keeps secure the chain of command between different organization subgroups and directs their energy toward legitimate organization goals. Without the social consensus and order that conformity helps to produce, organizational life would be difficult, if not unmanageably chaotic. The management of day-to-day affairs requires acceptance of some common rules of conduct. For that reason, whether they intend to or not, every human organization that survives, large or small, ultimately creates the means of developing and maintaining limits on the behavior and beliefs of its members.

Formal orientation programs and job training, casual conversation and the distillation of experience and observation teach organizational employees the rules to which they are expected to conform. In every organization there are do's and don'ts which cause employees to act in a predictable manner. Once in place, however, these do's and don'ts engage with a ruthless and relentless effort to survive. Because dissent challenges the validity of the do's and don'ts, questions the wisdom of existing technological, financial, and psychological investments, and threatens to undo the comfort of familiar work practices, it arouses anxiety and fear. In an effort to eliminate the cause of these unpleasant emotions, reassure themselves that their commitments and judgments are sound, and preserve their familiar, comfortable niche in the organization, organization employees, from the most senior to the most junior, commit ideacide by disregarding and often punishing those who dissent from the current consensus.

I want to tell you about what happened to the courageous managers from whom I gathered data. Their experiences, although frequently grim, actually form a thin, silver lining around the cloud which hangs about the management of courageous dissent in organizations.

Managers who act courageously experience one of three possible organizational responses: (1) **nothing**—the organization leaves them alone, neither rewarding nor punishing their effort; (2) **the organization rewards their effort**—they get a better job or some other perk that is a positively valued outcome; or (3) **the organization punishes their effort**—they are obliged to resign, are demoted, or experience some other outcome which they view as negative.

Forgetting for the moment whether their efforts succeeded or failed, after acting courageously nothing happened to 51% of the managers; another 29% enjoyed positive outcomes and the remaining 20% suffered negative ones. At first glance that pattern of organization response to courageous behavior may seem not too terrible. Neglect is the modal response. Unfortunately, as we unravel these gross findings it becomes evident that there is less to cheer about than first meets the eye.

To begin with, successful acts of managerial courage, those that do not suffer ideacide, are neither uniformly, nor even **mostly** rewarded. A minority of the courageous managers who were successful, 45%, experienced some form of positive organizational response. The slightly larger majority, however, 55%, report that they experienced **no** organizational response whatsoever—no promotions, salary increases or bonuses, not even a smiling "thank you." In contrast, punishment tends to be the organizational response to managers whose courageous acts were unsuccessful, having succumbed to ideacide. Fifty-six percent of them report that they were punished for simply having tried. The rest say, "Nothing happened."

So, 'tis a little better to succeed than to fail, but if you fail, take care. When a courageous initiative is rejected, more likely than not, the manager who advocated the idea will be punished. That is true regardless of the industry in which the manager is employed and no matter whether the courageous act was focused on business issues, superiors, subordinates, or ethical matters. The pervasiveness of this pattern should be a cause of concern for all of us. Clear evidence exists to show that by punishing those who courageously offer ideas, an organization chills the subsequent occurrence of managerial courage.

I asked managers how others behaved after witnessing courageous efforts. I was interested in the way organizational responses to managerial courage affected onlookers. In every instance where negative contagion occurred, that is, where courageous behavior **declined,** others in the organization witnessed the **punishment** of a courageous initiative which failed. A positive contagion of courageous behavior occurred when the initiative succeeded, regardless of whether it was followed by a positive organizational response or no response whatsoever. The conclusion is so obvious as to be embarrassing: Managers are influenced by what they see. More precisely, the absence of ideacide seems to be its own reward. If managers believe that ideas receive the proper attention, nothing more is necessary. Their willingness to engage in future acts of courage will not have been stilled. Courage is still-born, however, when an organization first commits ideacide, and then throws salt on the wound by also punishing the manager who courageously offered the idea. After witnessing someone else experience that sad combination of events, managers say, "Not me. I'll never behave courageously."

Please tolerate a brief digression for a good reason. I want to briefly explore the mass media's reporting of experiences that befall "whistleblowers" after they speak out. In so doing, I am making no claims about the courage of whistleblowers. Only one person in my sample falls into the category of people who speak out by going "public" and reporting alleged wrongdoing to either the media or "watchdog" groups, private and governmental. Therefore I have no firm empirical basis for knowing whether whistleblowers act from personal outrage or private vendetta. Whistleblowers are interesting to me because they are dissenters, and the mass media's presentation of their postwhistleblowing experiences is interesting to me because, inadvertently and through no fault of the media's, its reports may be deterring other forms of dissent in organizations, including managerial courage.

David Edwards, a recent and much celebrated whistleblower, is a native of Wichita Falls, Texas. In 1974, at the age of 30, he was in charge of *Les Cambiates*, the foreign exchange traders, for Citibank in Paris. A year later he charged the bank with tax evasion and currency trading violations. A *Fortune* magazine article by Roy Rowan, "The maverick who yelled foul at Citibank," reports that Edwards told his boss, his boss' bosses, and others in the Citibank hierarchy about his belief. All of them did the same thing, nothing.

The *Fortune* article said that Edwards "wasn't being prudish or picky about these foreign exchange abuses. That wouldn't have fit his high-noon, frontier personality. 'It's just bad business,' he kept telling his superiors."

One of these superiors reportedly told Edwards, "you get along by going along." Edwards couldn't go along so, in early 1978, he was fired.

Was he right? Did Citibank wander from a straight and narrow path? I don't know. Walter Wriston, former

Citibank chief executive officer, said that Edwards was fired because he "called his boss a crook" and turned down a job transfer. But some people evidently think otherwise. Citibank has had to pay $11 million in fines and back taxes to the governments of several countries and, in 1983, there was talk of collecting another $20 to $30 million. Also, in the United States, the Securities and Exchange Commission (SEC), which investigated the charges, said of this whistleblower:

> David Edwards was the individual in Citibank who made this case possible. He tried to get his suspicions investigated, and the questionable practices changed, and was fired for doing so. This agency and the U.S. government owe him a debt.

Let's consider the experience of a whistleblower who worked for the U.S. government as a Pentagon analyst, Franklin (Chuck) Spinney. Once, not so long ago, Spinney spoke to a special hearing of the Senate Armed Services Committee. Using data and Pentagon jargon, he spent two hours developing his case about the dangers and fallacies inherent in some aspects of defense planning and spending. Without a doubt, Spinney was risking his career by openly dissenting from established and accepted practice.

A *Time* magazine article describing Spinney's story quotes a colleague who describes Spinney as "dogged and thorough." He does his work with care and conviction and that has made Spinney "so troublesome in the eyes of his superiors that they have repeatedly tried to muzzle and several times to fire him." Do not be misled. Spinney is not antidefense. Of himself he said, "My view is that our country has to be strong and that we have to have the military assets to ensure that strength," and also "People have the idea that I'm out to find things wrong in the system, but that's just part of my job. There's no point in working on things that everyone agrees on, because that's not where the problems lie."

Spinney's reward for his effort was reported in an article in *The New York Times*, by Charles Mohr, on Friday, March 4, 1983. His ideas were unacceptable to others in the Pentagon. "He is no longer permitted computer access to budget data and he has been assigned to work in an entirely different area of study of 'deep strike interdiction' tactics by fighter bombers." The title of one article concerning this event offers a sad, final note, calling Franklin (Chuck) Spinney, "Pariah at the Pentagon." Such an outcome is hardly an invitation to dissent.

The potentially high price of dissent is also illustrated by the experience of a design engineer with the Defense Department, Ralph Applegate. Applegate noted that piston rings which cost civilians about $100, were costing the armed services $1130. Did applause go out to Applegate for trying to save taxpayers a bit more than $1000 per ring? Did he get a reward for trying?—say, the savings on just one of those rings? No, he didn't get the money, nor did he get praised. What he got was fired. He and others learned from this experience, they got the message, "You get along by going along."

The examples continue: George Geary, a sales executive for U.S. Steel, claims that he was fired because he told a government office about his reservations concerning the safety of new pipe. Daniel Gellert is a pilot with Eastern Airlines. In 1972 he argued that a design flaw in the automatic pilot system of the Tristar 1011 aircraft caused false readings about flight level when the plane was descending. Gellert claims that he was mistreated for presenting the case and is suing the airline for more than $1.5 million.

Five years before the Three Mile Island mishap occurred, Peter Faulkner, a systems application engineer for the Nuclear Services Corporation, claimed that power stations with serious design problems were being sold. Faulkner first tried to work within the company. He designed a system to detect flaws. But, he claims, no one cared. He went outside. Faulkner was fired in 1974.

In April 1973, Joseph Rose accepted a position as a corporate lawyer for the Associated Milk Producers, Inc. After discovering what he believed was evidence of illegal campaign contributions, he went to senior management. No response. So he gathered the evidence and tried to see the organization's board. The result: "He claims that the next day he found a new lock on his office door and a guard posted there to keep him out. He was subsequently fired."

Organizations do not suffer whistleblowers lightly. They are commonly treated as subversives whose only aim is to undermine the system. For their "crimes" they are punished, typically by expulsion. My aim in this diagnosis is not to defend whistleblowers. I make no claims about their courage, altruism, or accuracy. My primary concern is with acts of dissent in organizations. If whistleblowing is an extreme example of dissent, then it may be true that the magnitude of organizational response, expulsion, is atypical. But even if the magnitude is atypical, the fact of a negative organizational response following unacceptable, rejected proposals seems very typical. Moreover, and most important, I think that there is every reason to believe that the public awareness of this response has a chilling effect on all dissent in organizations, including acts of managerial courage.

Additional evidence about the effects of positive and negative organizational responses to successful and unsuccessful acts of managerial courage comes from the courageous managers themselves. I asked them, "Would you do it again?" Eighty-four percent of those whose courageous efforts succeeded in getting a hearing said "yes," as compared to 67% of managers whose efforts failed under the crush of ideacide. The picture grows more dim still when we examine a manager's willingness to courageously offer new ideas on some future occasion. Of those who were treated positively (they also succeeded), 100% said that they would do it again. In contrast, 75% of those who experienced some negative response (they also failed) said, "No. Not me. Not again."

An organization's response to acts of managerial courage acts as a valve, regulating the future flow of courage in the organization. Balance is the key. If an organization closes the valve too tightly, by either committing idea-

cide or punishing the managers who dared, then courageous initiative will be reduced to a trickle, and the
organization will languish in a desert of conformity.

The extreme opposite response to acts of managerial
courage seems no better as a solution to the organization's
interminable dilemma of choosing between the forces of
continuity and discontinuity. For, if the valve is opened
too widely, by either declining to punish anyone regardless of the substance of their dissent or noncontingent
reward of any courageous act, regardless of its acceptability, then the organization is likely to be drowned in a
flood of courageous chaos.

Balance is the key and a principle organizational tool
for maintaining balance is an organization's total response
to acts of managerial courage. Properly employed, in
ways that I discuss in Chapter 8, this tool can move the
organization safely between conformity and chaos. Pressures arising from both the practical realities of introducing change and the conservative-tending psychology of
human groups may be unavoidable, but they are not un-
manageable. The first step is diagnosis. Conscious attention to the occurrence and causes of ideacide allows
organizations to therapeutically adjust their responses in
this endless struggle. In an effort to further diagnostic insight, the next chapter identifies four key organizational
conditions which artifically and unnecessarily strengthen
the natural tides tugging in the direction of ideacide.

Chapter Four

Ideacide: The Major Culprits

"There's a Right Way To Do Things Around Here"

Organizations that place special emphasis on either hierarchy or harmony, those which, by design or accident, use **reward structures** that praise followers and punish leaders, and those which embrace values expressing an **irrational faith in rationality,** all strengthen the natural drift toward ideacide, elevating conformity and stifling managerial courage. The 200-plus managers I questioned alerted me to the importance of these four culprits and their impact on organization life. Their observations offer important diagnostic insight to anyone who wants to stimulate the flow of ideas in his or her own organization.

Hierarchy

Hierarchically inclined organizations that stress strict adherence to rules and deferential obedience to roles can be perversely creative, and tragically comical in the means that they devise to stifle courageous initiative. An internal consultant and management educator with whom I worked for 15 years was fond of asking managers for "idea killers," that is, typical organizational responses to new ideas and creative suggestions. Some of the most common "idea killers" that I heard managers report to him were:

The boss won't like it.

It's not policy.

I don't have the authority.

We're not in the (fill in with the name of any industry **other than** the organization's) business.

Does (fill in with a competitor's name) do it?

Too much risk.

It's not **my** job (or **your** job, or **their** job).

Not invented here (NIH).

It's never been tried.

We've always done it this way.

There's no precedent.

It's not in the budget.

Why rock the boat?

Send it to committee!

Idea killers are the handmaidens of continuity. They are the symptoms of an addiction to established procedure and the current consensus.

Acts of managerial courage are the essence of organizational discontinuity. They are surprising, controversial, and rule breaking, all the things that hierarchically oriented bureaucracy abhors. For generations, scholars have noted that bureaucratic hierarchies foster, thrive, and survive on continuity. Max Weber, the venerable dean of this group, characterized bureaucracies as seeking precision, reliability, and efficiency. In order to accomplish these ends, noted the famed sociologist Robert Merton, bureaucracies want their official members to conform to rules and regulations. Methodical, predictable obedience to routine procedure is essential for bureaucratic success. Bureaucracies are not at all fond of exceptional solutions to problems. As one more recent scholar noted, they want a "roster of familiar strategies" to solve problems. In bureaucracies, ideally speaking, rules should regulate conduct, thereby providing control and consistency of individual behavior. Everyone will "do it by the book" and, if the book is suited to the existing demands of the business environment, success should follow. Unfortunately, the environment isn't always so obliging.

A poor fit between the business environment of the 1980s and the traditional style of German management may be contributing to the current troubles of industry in West Germany, according to an article in *The Wall Street Journal*. In the 1960s and 1970s, the style of West German managers suited business needs: "Their cautious, technical approach made them the ideal captains of the heavy manufacturing industries that formed the powerful base of Germany's postwar economy." But times pass and conditions change. Now

As German executives and management consultants take stock, they discern a worrisome aloofness and rigidity at the top of many German companies—a lack of flexibility that some see imperiling Germany's ability to remain a lasting rival to U.S. and Japanese industry.

Part of the problem is attributed to the *Vorstand*, the managing board of German companies. Its members talk to each other, maintain peer relationships and even engage in consensual decision making among themselves. Their dealings with the company employees seems very different. According to the article, others perceive them as aloof, remote, rigid, and unreceptive to new ideas. It may have worked at one time, but no longer does. There is a need for change.

For different reasons, the same statement can be made about the management of industry in the Soviet Union. A *New York Times* article discussed a memo prepared by a group of Soviet economists from the Siberian division of the Academy of Sciences in Novosibirsk. The memo was concerned with the cause of low levels of production. What did they conclude was the single greatest hindrance to production? Investment? Raw materials availability or their costs? Delivery or distribution systems? The weather? No, no, no, and no again! Their conclusion was bureaucracy, rigidly centralized controls developed with a system over 50 years old and perpetuated despite its poor fit with modern conditions.

The actual report, as translated in the article, says, "Within the framework of that system, people were regarded as 'cogs' in the economic mechanism, and they behaved accordingly—obediently (passively), like machines and material." Note carefully the words "obediently" and "passively," for they are simple substitutes for "conformity" and "noncourageous behavior." Individual initiative and challenge are stifled in a system that is so tightly controlled.

The "core of skilled workers" the report claimed, "were better educated, capable of 'critically assessing the activities of political and economic leaders' and of 'standing up for themselves.' " The managing bureaucrats were unresponsive to these potentials, pursuing instead their system of tight, central controls.

Although none of the American managers that I questioned reported that they worked in anything like a Soviet bureaucracy, their answers to a question about what organizational conditions stifle managerial courage contain some obvious similarities. More than half described conditions which are readily identified as characteristics of an autocratically managed, bureaucratic hierarchy. For example, some said that the management style was "top-down; dominant; intimidating." Referring to the matter of organizational structure they said that organizations which stifle courage are "centrally organized with limited local authority." Or, such organizations have "restricted delegation of authority for expenditures." Some managers simply said that the major obstacle was "bureaucracy— that is, corporate constraint through defined authority limits." The kinds of operating business systems which prevent courageous behavior were described in the same manner: "highly structured planning, financial systems," "highly formalized reporting, planning accounting systems," "strict policy on prior approvals," "tight controls," "company bound by policy, procedure," and "policy and procedure guide [behavior] above judgment."

General comments about the climate of a stifling organization continue to portray a rigid, autocratic hierarchy, tolerating little or no dissent: "reinforcement of obedience to orders from above," "fear of authority," "fear of displeasing supervisor—negative appraisal," "fear of reprisal for not playing by the rules," "safest way to progress is to do what supervisor wants," "intolerance of failure in business development effort," "lack of reward for risk taking," "low risk climate," "insubordination punished," and "Standard Operating Procedure (SOP) is eleventh commandment."

When senior management is inclined to operate the business in an autocratic, bureaucratically oriented way, the pressures against managerial initiative can be enormous. An illustration is contained in the following excerpt, which is actually a composite of two interviews with managers who operated in that type of environment in two different companies.

COMPOSITE: The event occurred while I was attending a meeting where planners from one of our companies were going to make a presentation—at the time I was corporate financial planning manager.

H.H.: Who else was at the meeting?

COMPOSITE: Senior executives including the CEO of my group—two levels above me—other senior people, her level and above, as well as mine—35 to 40 people all together.

H.H.:   What happened?

COMPOSITE: Well I had a job to do. It was my responsibility
to question, query. You know, test the validity
of assumptions and conclusions. The truth is I
believed that the presenters were right—their
conclusions—even though I wondered about
the analysis.

Charlie Purdy, the CEO of my group, took
off after them. He was giving them a terrible
time. There was lots of silence, tension. He was
very angry—against their position.

I found myself even almost astonished to
hear my voice—speaking up—with a great deal
of trepidation, saying [to Mr. Purdy] that while
I was prepared to question assumptions, I went
to the area on your behalf, Mr. Purdy, and I became convinced that what they have concluded
is the proper recommendation.

My boss got furious with me. He said, "I
don't care what your thoughts are. What you're
saying is all well and good—but it's not what I'm
looking for." Then, later in his office he said,
"You didn't get the proper signal. There's a way
to do things around here. You follow the book
and that wasn't by the book. You should have
kept your mouth shut."

In the kind of autocratically managed bureaucracy that
this composite interview excerpt typifies, "you get along
by going along." And going along does not include con-
tradicting your boss, or questioning rules.

This stifling organizational creed brings to mind the

experiences of another manager from whom I collected data. She explained that, after her courageous effort failed, she was put on "special assignment." And what is a "special assignment?" Well, in her words, "a special assignment is a morgue for unsuccessful courageous managers." Can anyone really doubt that retaliatory consequences of this sort produce a chilling effect on subordinate willingness to speak out?

Some claim that the consequences of such a chill are evident in ITT's fate during Harold Geneen's tenure and after his departure. Richard Pascale and Anthony Athos describe the style of this most controversial executive in their book, *The Art of Japanese Management.* One way in which Geneen maintained control was through a network of informants. For example, he used staff departments as a kind of check and balance on line operations. They kept watch and informed Geneen if the line people wandered from the game plan; "at the center of the whole thing sat Geneen, watching for evidence someone wasn't doing what **he** would do if he were there." Pascale and Athos advance the view that Geneen wanted carbon copies of himself, servile reflections who followed the game plan, his, doing what he would do. When employees failed to follow his lead, the response was dramatically clear. "What is to a degree unusual was that Geneen did not seek to diminish what he deplored, he sought to eliminate it. This driving will to determine the behavior of his subordinates was single-minded . . . Mr. Geneen simply fired or humiliated those who were not performing according to his plan."

For a time, ITT grew and then it faltered. The causes of its faltering are undoubtedly multiple—as are the causes of its growth—but one which some observers identify is management's inability to exercise ingenuity and remain flexibly innovative in managing the enterprise.

Henry Ford was not Harold Geneen, but he is someone to whom a patriarchal, controlling, "I'll brook no argument," style of management is attributed. The innovations of specialization and progressive production that he introduced into manufacturing in the early 1900s were momentous. But, in time, innovation was replaced by inertia in a corporate environment that was, in all likelihood, chilled by his style. And, along came GM, Alfred Sloan, coordination by committee, and decentralization. Sloan described his company's pummeling of Ford in his autobiography, *My Years with General Motors.*

> The rise of the closed body made it impossible for Mr. Ford to maintain his leading position in the low-priced field, for he had frozen his policy in the Model T, and the Model T was pre-eminently an open-car design. (Actually some change occurred and Ford had some closed cars produced, but nothing like the number that the market wanted.) . . . The old master had failed to master change.

It's a common problem with old **masters**! Ford, the old master, was firmly in control. That was the beginning of the Ford story and was also very nearly its end. The Model T fell and Ford lost its position in the industry to GM for many years to follow.

It was a different story in 1980 when Donald E. Petersen, the recently appointed president of Ford Motor Company, visited the corporate styling center to preview clay models of future car designs. Sensing unhappiness, Petersen asked the designers if they liked what they were presenting.

John Holusha, who reported this event in *The New York Times*, tells us that the designers answered, "No," they weren't satisfied. The event led Petersen and Ford CEO, Phillip Caldwell, to give the designers greater freedom in developing design, a freedom which did not exist before since, as we were told, the designers were too worried about **meeting their boss' desires.** "Out of that freedom has come the smooth, uncluttered, sleekly aerodynamic look of Ford's new models, a sharp departure from the square, formal appearance of its older cars—and from everyone else's designs too." Hooray for Petersen and Caldwell. In this instance, at least, they understood that it's difficult for a company to be a leader in the industry if its key people feel obliged to slavishly follow the hierarchy's game plan. Petersen and Caldwell gave the designers the support that they needed in order to experiment and innovate.

The managers from whom I collected data did not typically feel the level of support from their higher-ups that the Ford designers experienced on that occasion in 1980. When I asked them how their superiors responded to their courageous efforts, only one-third reported support while the remaining two-thirds said that their bosses were either opposed (about 45%) or not involved (about 20%). Evidently, managers who decide to act courageously should expect do so without support from up above. What they can expect from their own subordinates is completely different.

Of the managers, 71% said that their subordinates supported their courageous acts, while only 29% said that their subordinates were either "not involved" (25%) or opposed (4%). That's a nearly perfect reversal of the pattern for higher-ups. Is it too cynical to say that this is true to form: those higher up in the organization protected the status quo or their own flanks while those lower down were obedient to the hierarchy and simply conformed to their bosses' game plans.

Unsurprisingly, who supports a courageous act has a dramatic impact on the likelihood that it will meet with ideacide. Overall, 65% of my managers report that their ideas successfully gained a satisfactory hearing. If they can claim support of subordinates that figure jumps to 73%. Not bad, but it doesn't compare to what happens if they are able to say that their immediate boss supported them, in which case the percentage of success leaps to 90. And, if they are lucky enough to have the support of superiors other than their immediate boss, then the percentage of success is a perfect 100; none suffered failure because of ideacide.

What is support worth in terms of the organization's treatment of managers who succeed or fail? A lot. If subordinates support a manager's courageous act, then failure may be accompanied by some negative consequences: Of this group, 9% were demoted, fired, or pressured to resign. If bosses or other superiors support the effort, however, that never happens. Not one manager with support from higher-ups reported experiencing any negative treatment by the organization. That's power, and it communicates an unforgettable message to managers about when to speak out courageously and when to remain safely silent: If you lack support of the hierarchy, then there is considerable danger in dissenting from the game plan. The sad part is that if you decide to dissent from the game plan, hierarchical support is somewhat improbable. By regulating the valve of organizational response in this way, organizations inclined toward bureaucratic hierarchy stifle courage and produce the strict adherence to rules and regulations that they so suicidally desire.

The likelihood of a courageous idea's success or failure was also affected by a manager's position in the organization hierarchy at the time that he or she spoke out. But the pattern may not be exactly what you expect.

The people from whom I gathered data were placed into one of four categories. In ascending order, the first three of these were: (1) supervisors—first and second level, (2) unit or department heads, and (3) general managers or executives. The last category of people, a group that I call "individual contributors" don't really fit neatly into the hierarchy so let's deal with them first. They succeeded all of the time. Their expertise and position as a unique organizational resource placed them in a special role vis-à-vis others. Few could exercise authority over them on technical matters, and most were generally constrained in employing any coercive tactics for fear of losing a valuable and often highly marketable resource.

The fate of the others is not so rosy. The supervisors do okay. Of that group 92% were successful. But it's downhill as you move up the organizational ladder. Unit and department heads succeeded 65% of the time and general managers and executives only 50% of the time.

Are you surprised to learn that chances of success decrease as you move up the organizational hierarchy? I'm not, and I'll tell you why in a bit, after I report some additional information which makes it clear what this pattern does **not** say. The apparently logical extension of this pattern is not valid. People at the **lowest levels** of an organization are not the most successful when it comes to courageous behavior. Using questionnaires, I asked an additional 47 blue-collar employees to tell me about their courageous behavior. They were all members of the same union in the same company, the majority being unskilled laborers. Only nine of these people (19%) reported acting courageously and five of the nine reported failure.

One person's comments, more than any of the numbers, captures for me this group's experiences with courageous behavior. The man was an unmarried, 24-year-old porter. I'll call his company Bolt. "In the Bolt Company caurageous [sic] behavior is not in the rule book! If it is not in the rule book, we are not permited [sic] to do it."

But why did you do it, he was asked. His reply was "There are times when you as a person has to do what you know is right."

And what happened to you and the organization afterward? "If the Bolt Company found out, there [sic] procedure would be to give you a commodation [sic] and a caution both in the same breath. Dammed [sic] if you do, dammed [sic] if you don't."

Publishing customs compel me to identify spelling errors with the word *sic*, but the man's eloquence does not really deserve the presence of such minor distractions. His words, and the data that his fellows provided, should disabuse anyone of the false notion that those at the bottom of an organization have the easiest time behaving courageously.

Nonetheless, it is the case that as we move from supervisors up to general managers and executives, success in courageous behavior is less, not more likely. Why? Aren't people higher in the hierarchy more powerful, freer to do what they want? The simple answer is "no," that is not so obviously true. It is, of course, true that as you move up the hierarchy the power to influence greater numbers of people is legitimately yours. But is it not clear that a manager is free to exercise that power in any way that he or she chooses. Actions of more senior people are more visible ("set an example" they are told) and more consequential, and the pressure from powerful peers (who often have conflicting interests to one's own), superiors, and even from one's own subordinates, may be on maintaining continuity rather than flirting with discontinuity. In many ways, senior members of the hierarchy, more than junior ones, are expected to uphold, not deviate, from the bureaucratic game plan.

In Orangeburg, New York, for example, in 1981, a recession year, some senior executives at Material Resource Corporation (MRC) were concerned that their chairman, Sheldon Weinig, was making a mistake. In 1957 MRC was founded by Weinig. It produced coatings which, according to a *New York Times* article by Stan Luxenberg, were "used to make integrated circuits in the semiconductor and computer industries." Metals for the coatings were also processed by MRC. In 1981 the company had about 700 employees and had previously earned a net income of $2.3 million on $71 million sales. During that year its sales would fall to $10 million and its net income to $728,000. If the company fired 100 workers who were no longer required, it would realize a savings of almost $4 million.

Weinig rejected conventional wisdom and the advice of his subordinates. He kept all the workers on the payroll. He even repeated an earlier pledge that no one at MRC would ever be laid off. His reasoning? Well, apparently for Weinig it was a long-term investment—good business. It would produce loyalty to the company by skilled, knowledgeable employees.

"Mr. Weinig faced constant criticism. Stockholders lectured him on his responsibility to maximize profits." Their concerns were not unjustified. The company's stock plummeted in 1981 from $36 per share to $12.50. "Some workers were worried that Mr. Weinig was jeopardizing the company. The financial vice-president, Garrett Pierce, argued the program put a strain on MRC." Weinig persisted. If he was wrong it might have cost him dearly.

People were reassigned, often to lesser jobs, without paycuts. Security and cleaning were handled internally instead of by outside contractors. Underutilized technical people made calls on customers that the rush of work had always prevented. Weinig persisted. In 1983 business picked up. Normal work assignments were resumed. Weinig had prevailed, MRC was ready for the upturn— the staff was generally intact.

With all due respect, Weinig was a corporate maverick and a courageous leader. True, he had clout, but he was also vulnerable. He persisted through a storm of opposition. Remember your responsibility, he was told. There was a safer route for Weinig. One hundred fewer employees was worth $4 million to MRC. Anyone following the conventional, conservative bureaucratic game plan would not have made Weinig's choice. Weinig did not succumb, but the fact that he is such an exception proves the rule: the uniqueness of his experience illustrates how, in most other organizational circumstances, bureaucracies create followers, ultimately denuding an organization of courage and leadership, and destroying its potential for regeneration.

In bureaucratic, hierarchical organizations, obedience to job-related power and the letter of the institution's rules is paramount no matter what level you occupy. Managerial courage is contrary. It challenges routine and established practice, the very essence of this kind of organization. It is a heresy requiring exorcism.

The excesses and unwelcome by-products of bureaucracy and autocratic hierarchy have been recognized for some time. One response to these deficits has been to orient organizations toward more harmonious, cooperative, team like arrangements, stressing informality and participation, and blurring distinctions among employees. Even under these seemingly idyllic circumstances, however, it is evident that acts of managerial courage become heresies needing exorcism.

Harmony

In an effort to achieve harmony, groups often homogenize individual behavior and opinion into an undifferentiated, pale, inoffensive substance. In this way, consensus replaces diversity as a characteristic of the group's life. The formation of this homogenized pap must be aided when individual differences are pressured together by an organization's well-intended injunction to be harmonious. Through a succession of concessions, prompted by the desire to avoid conflict and achieve harmony, each person yields a little so that the agreements which finally result are no one's and everyone's. What often emerges under the pressure to get along, be nice, and work and play well together is an uncontroversial package of rules about how to act and what to think, distinguished only by their blandness.

A work group which has evolved in this way is bound to view the individual pursuit of social approval through conformity to group opinion and practice as a "good" to be rewarded. It strengthens feelings of group harmony. It provides stability, predictability, and order. It ignites in other group members a warm sense of cohesion and an affirmation that what they are doing is right. It symbolically embraces group norms and values. And it may be the kiss of death because, ultimately, the process set in motion by the organization's injunction to be harmonious exacerbates the natural drift toward ideacide, stifling individual acts of managerial courage.

Alexis de Tocqueville, that extraordinary man who so carefully observed the birth of the United States two centuries ago, was also deeply concerned about conformity. He spoke of it as the "tyranny of the majority." De Tocqueville believed that, in time, the United States risked the prevention of free expression of opinion not by law or the force of arms, but by the action of subtle social forces spurred on by the commitment to social equality. His concern about equality fostering a tyranny of the majority is shared by managers who worked in settings where, in the hope of achieving harmony, stress was placed on a leveling of differences, on being "one of the boys," "just a big happy family—no chiefs—all equals." The reasoning is simple: Differences in prestige and power are potentially divisive, therefore let's pretend that they do not exist. This egalitarian tendency is fed, in the United States and in U.S. organizations, by the customary informality between people. De Tocqueville's comments on American society, therefore, contain rich insight for managers in any organization intent on minimizing hierarchical distinctions. He said:

> For as conditions became more equal, Americans seemed more and more to take pride not in their individuality, in their personal liberties, in their freedom, but rather in their sameness. [In the end] . . . every citizen, being assimilated to all the rest, is **lost in the crowd,** and nothing stands conspicuous but the great and imposing image of the people at large.

When the social process in organizations places a high value on everyone being the same, just another one of the gang, the tyranny which follows has the capacity to "chill innovators, and to keep them silent and at a respectful distance" (de Tocqueville). Thus, in organizations, as in political life, the effects of equality are potentially double-edged. They are obstacles to autocracy (the tyranny of a **minority,**) but they enhance conformity (the tyranny of the **majority.**).

De Tocqueville's view about the individual psychological dynamics that feed a tyranny of the majority is explained when he says:

> As men grow more alike, each man feels himself weaker in regard to all the rest; as he discerns nothing by which he is considerably raised above them, or distinguished from them, he mistrusts himself as soon as

they assail him. . . . [Thus] The majority do not need to constrain him; they convince him.

Mind what I am saying. Do not close this book charging me with a wholesale condemnation of harmony or egalitarian practices in organizations. Such is not my belief nor is it the implication of this research. The benefits of greater harmony and more egalitarian conditions in organizations are many, but they do not come free of charge. There are potential costs against which organizations must guard. I am simply sounding the alarm.

I am certain that A.J., who is a marketing manager in a retail firm, understands why the alarm needs to be raised. "How did others respond to your efforts?" I asked him.

Others couldn't understand why I didn't—wouldn't fit in. They said, "It's easier to fit in. Why don't you play the game. You're too rigid, constrained." I never heard that before.

They wanted me to join their happy little club where being pleasant meant more than being productive. To heck with that. It was a quality circle that had no quality. They were friendly, but in terms of the organization—why we were there—no quality.

The true character of organizations implied by A.J.'s response to my question is more completely described in the questionnaire responses of many other managers. In responding to the inquiry about what organization conditions discourage courageous managerial behavior, approximately one-third of them pointed to a deliberate organizational emphasis on harmony and egalitarian conditions as the principle cause. In one fashion or another, many of this group said that pressure to maintain cohesiveness stifled courage. Some spoke of a "premium placed on solidarity," "the discomfort of being distinct," "an over-emphasis on consensus," and the "pressure to maintain a consensus—even a false one." Many other responses reflected the same theme with different words: "pressure to maintain a happy family atmosphere of not criticizing policy, procedure, or company," "don't rock the boat," "team work/committee environment," "no individual action wanted—appreciated," "a fraternal climate," and "informal culture—don't break step with the troops."

Thus, as common social denominators are found and alikeness is produced and organizationally endorsed, the basis for courage is undermined. Individual acts of managerial courage often require "breaking step with the troops." They challenge popular, established practices and familiar routines. Courageous initiatives frequently spark conflict, disrupting organizational harmony. Such conflict is one of the principal organizational benefits of managerial courage. When properly managed, conflict focuses choices, aids commitment, elevates thinking, and sharpens issues. Productive conflict, by continually juxtaposing organizational options, can be an enormous aid to organizational growth and progress. Conformity-driven compromise, produced by individual self-censoring and group homogenizing of ideas which might cause dissension, ultimately leaves organizations without the option of choosing radically new pathways into the future. Thus, through different processes the outcomes produced by some efforts to maintain harmony are no less dangerous to organization regeneration than those outcomes which occur because employees are intimidated by a rigid and punishing autocratic bureaucracy.

In the light of evidence provided by others, these findings about the effects of harmony on managerial courage trouble me. From the mid-1950s until very recently, scholars have been alarmed at the inroads being made by a social ethic which espouses groups, not individuals, as the prime source of creativity and proclaims group membership, an experience akin to being in a family, as the ultimate need of an individual.

Almost 20 years after Whyte published *The Organization Man,* challenging this social ethic, in an article in the *Harvard Business Review,* Abraham Zaleznik observed, "Business has established a new power ethic that favors collective over individual leadership, the cult of the group over that of personality." It's all part of a trend. Outside organizations there are communes, encounter groups, religious cults, and self-help groups of every sort. Inside organizations we have teams, committees, task forces, ad hoc groups, steering committees, and quality circles. Is it any wonder that in a 1980 issue of *Organization Dynamics,* the well-known organizational psychologist Harold Leavitt and his coauthor, Jean Blumen-Lipman, looked at this burgeoning array of social gatherings and concluded that the "hunger for warm, affectionate relationships appears to be growing in the United States."

Whether the hunger is greater I do not know, but the proliferation troubles me because I believe my data: Groups have a capacity for producing a special, perniciously subtle tyranny. The ascendance of the social ethic, the priority being placed on both maintaining harmony and working through social consensus, and the swelling endorsement of teams as a means of getting work done, all augur poorly for individual acts of managerial courage and organization regeneration. Whyte illustrated the dilemma when he wrote, "Finding a middleway in conflicts of interest between the group and oneself has always been difficult, but it has become particularly difficult as people have come to believe there should be, ideally, no conflicts. . . . " Echoing Whyte's thoughts, one manager said to me, "Participate, one is encouraged, but in a way that the group approves. Offer ideas, but keep them within the ball park. Challenge, but not too severely."

Autocrats who pound their desks demanding conformity to rules and scaring the devil out of nearly everyone are probably detested universally. The problems that they cause are understood and, for two or three decades, more progressive organizations have undertaken remedial efforts of ever-increasing social/psychological sophistication. However, these efforts themselves contain elements which present a new danger. The warmly embracing organizational demands for egalitarianism, harmony, and social consensus can be as violently coercive to individuals as the menacing gestures of a desk-pounding autocrat. Despite their many differences, a rigid organizational endorsement of either bureaucratic hierarchy or leveling, social harmony share one profoundly important desire: They both prefer conforming followers to courageous leaders. The realization of that desire furthers organization degeneration and retards the progress of any national industrial renewal.

Rewards

It is possible, perhaps even common, for men and women to climb the managerial ladder by responding only to immediate pressures and short-term goals; by seeking cautious compromise; by striking expedient agreements with friends and foes; by following orders, obediently and without question; by lubricating the system with diplomatic, Machiavellian, and financial grease in order to avoid fundamental change; and even by coercing subordinates through intimidation and punishment. It is possible to find successful managers who do all these things, but make certain that when you count their number you do not make the mistake of categorizing any one of them as a leader. None challenges what is with visions of what might be. None produces creative new directions for an organization, firing the passions and work efforts of other employees. None voices courageous options which, if they do not break the organizational mold, at least require some fundamental realignment of its basic contours.

Managers who ascend the corporate ladder because they are compromising, cautious, and conforming are followers. They are essential to the successful maintenance of day-to-day organization operation, for they keep the system functioning smoothly, consistently, and predictably. Without these people organizational stability and equilibrium are threatened. They are the best reason to respect the forces of continuity, but they are **not** leaders.

Leaders guide, they go in advance of, enrich, empower, elevate, correct, and occasionally ignore the superficial roar of surrounding opinion. If they do less, then they are an echo, a thoughtless imitation, lacking novelty or purpose, sometimes loud, but always destined to quickly fade into an unmarked, organizational oblivion.

Some years ago, pursuing his interest in leaders, Warren Bennis conducted a study of 90 CEOs, which included in-depth interviews of 10 who were identified as innovative. One of the things most characteristic of these CEOs was that they were concerned with purpose and direction, not with daily how to's. As Bennis described it, they placed emphasis on doing the right thing, not on doing things right.

Leaders who are concerned with doing the right things step out beyond immediate pressure and passion to envision and articulate beneficial alternatives to the status quo. The real hero of James MacGregor Burns' *Leadership*, the "transforming leader," is such a person:

> The transforming leader looks for potential motives in followers, seeks to satisfy **higher** needs, and engages the full person of the follower. The result of transforming leadership is a relationship of mutual stimulation and elevation that converts followers into leaders and may convert leaders into moral agents.

Courage is an indispensable ingredient of leadership. By going beyond what **is**, by seeking what might **be**, the right thing to do, managers become leaders. They ask fundamental questions about the appropriateness and efficacy of established practice, and in so doing they jeopardize their own welfare, for social ire, not inspiration, is often the final and most consequential outcome of their effort.

Followers are deterred by that awesome possibility. They prefer to tread on a safer path. But, "leaders, whatever their professions of harmony, do not shun conflict, they confront it, exploit it, ultimately **embody** it." Leaders are willing to make enemies. They must, as Burns so eloquently says, be willing "to deny themselves the affection of adversaries."

Courage, conflict, and leadership are on intimate terms. It is hard to imagine organization regeneration without them. Courageous expression of alternatives penetrates organization inertia, producing a sharpened awareness of differences in either interests or values, and therefore conflict. When managed productively rather than destructively, the conflict signals trouble and may stimulate remedy; it invigorates, creating fresh energy for work; and it stretches imagination, producing new ideas, innovations, and creative integration of intraorganizational diversity.

Leaders are active, not reactive. Their efforts are personal, intimate, and invested with emotional energy. Managers/followers gingerly navigate their way through the system. Courageous leaders shock the system. Filled with passion, their efforts pursue alternatives to established practice, accepting conflict as a legitimate instrument of organization regeneration. Unlike followers, leaders aspire to the unprecedented, experiment with the unfamiliar, and embrace the unpopular.

Unfortunately, the tide of organizational life commonly flows against such behavior. Despite passionate pleas for leadership, courage, initiative, outspokenness, creativity, and lateral thinking, some 10% of the managers whom I questioned said that formal and informal organizational reward systems exerted steady pressure on them to eschew the unprecedented, the unfamiliar, and the unpopular. Rather, they felt pressed into maintaining a self-protective, short-term outlook. A revealing example of how this occurs was contained in an interview that I did with a production manager of an oil refinery.

> The new refinery manager was on his way up. He was favored by whoever—you know, anointed. Anyway, in

this atmosphere he wanted to control costs. That way he'd look good. He had his eyes focused on a year, maybe 18 months ahead. For him this was a very temporary assignment. That's the problem for all of us— it's temporary, so no one really cares long term. You don't have to live with the consequences. So maybe some people try to do nothing, avoid difficulty, risks, expenses, anything that may be trouble—look bad— while they are accountable. To hell with what happens after they go. It's true right to the top of the organization. Today is what counts. You don't get promoted because of what happens tomorrow, when you're gone. That's how the system works.

Anyway, the story is that this fellow is going to look good by cutting into maintenance. It's common. You make it look like you've done something, but really keep it to a minimum. Don't do anything that would shut down production. The problem is that maintenance needs don't go away. Eventually the equipment goes, then you can have big trouble. But what you hope is that it's someone else's trouble.

Anyway, when his strategy was clear I decided to back the maintenance manager—he was already complaining. You see it's really **his** business [Note: said sarcastically]—I don't really **think that way, but** if I were like that—you know—look after my own affairs, I wouldn't say anything. No one points the finger at me if maintenance is lacking. Anyway, I can't be that way. It's not how I work. You have to have pride in doing things right. So I spoke to the refinery manager. I knew he didn't like to hear what I had to say, but he was polite. I knew he wasn't going to change and told him it wasn't satisfactory. We argued. Some things got patched up. Just enough—you know. He moved on in a while and—it was almost funny if it weren't so sad— his replacement was barely on the job—in his office— when, **blooey,** we had to shut the whole thing down.

This example is particularly disturbing because the allegedly short-sighted refinery manager was not turning his back on bold ingenuity and innovation, he was rejecting what seems to have been essential and ordinary equipment maintenance in order to fashion for himself an unblemished corporate image and ensure promotion. It's tempting to place the entire blame on this fellow, charging him with all sorts of moral flaws and deficits of character, but that seems too one-sided. I share the observation of the production manager who told me the story: "Today is what counts. You don't get promoted because of what happens tomorrow—when you're gone. *That's how the system works.*"

Often organizations inadvertently encourage employees to become followers and practice management by retreat, **MBR:** When in doubt never advance, protect your flanks, move to an area of safety, a position that can be easily defended. As a strategy, **MBR** is understandably prudent for the individual manager inasmuch as it increases the odds on his or her survival. But when **MBR** is practiced by most managers, because it is institutionally rewarded, organizational survival is in danger of suffocating under a tide of self-serving caution.

Rationality

The impetus to substitute self-serving caution for courage may have been boosted in recent years by what some identify as a growing tendency for managers to be obsessively methodical and excessively rational in decision making. Such claims come from several quarters. Zaleznik has commented on the occurrence of this tendency, saying:

> A technologically oriented and economically successful society tends to deprecate the need for great leaders. Such societies hold a deep and abiding faith in rational methods of solving problems, including problems of value, economics and justice.

In everyday practice, this irrational faith in rationality ushers into organizational life a most incredible paradox, one that was insightfully observed by Thomas J. Peters and Robert H. Waterman, Jr., in their best seller, *In Search of Excellence.* They illustrate how new ideas and necessary action are put on "hold" as everyone waits for **the numbers,** whose magical powers people imagine will produce solutions to any problem. Following **MBR,** managers cling to the credo that **ambiguity requires inaction,** or as Peters and Waterman call it, "paralysis through analysis."

"Analyze, wait for forecasts, calculate d.c.f.'s, quantify—above all, quantify—that's the key to control, and control is what it's all about," one manager told me. She complained that she and others were pressured into pretending that the business environment, inside and outside the organization, was completely controllable and totally predictable. If anything went wrong, she said, then the accusation was "you haven't done your homework." Almost 10% of the managers I questioned agreed that this organizational misplacement of faith in rationality was the fourth major culprit causing ideacide.

It is foolish to be only harshly critical of this trend in organization life. The benefits are clear: **Whim** and bias are frequently replaced by information and accuracy. But it would be equally foolish to pretend that all the numbers that are needed to make a decision are always available, or that even when they are available in substantial quantity, their interpretation is regularly unambiguous. Decision making in organizations cannot be reduced to a precise algebra, emptied of the subjective sway of human forces. If it could, then organizations would have fewer problems and I would have no book to write.

The fact is that strict adherence to the rational model often restricts adaptive exploration and devalues experimentation in the absence of a nearly irrefutable, empirical, advance guarantee of success, a demand that is simply too great given our level of knowledge about marketplace dynamics. And who or what is to blame for this state of affairs? It is hard to confidently point an accusing finger at any one cause. Certainly there is merit in Zaleznik's concern about the technological and scientific orientation of many modern societies, whereby all problems are imagined to be solvable through rational means. Others have pointed their fingers at business schools as the institutions that have done the most to promote this dysfunctional level of methodicalness and rationality in corporate life.

During the spring of 1984, 1000 graduates of Stanford University's Graduate School of Business met for two days at New York City's posh Hotel Pierre. Among the speakers who appeared before them was professor of organizational behavior Harold J. Leavitt. The concern of his presentation was with what he identified as a misemphasis in management education. In order to explain the misemphasis, Leavitt described three categories of managers. **Type three** managers, he said, are **doers.** They get things done by dealing with people. Psychologists, salespeople, and attorneys are all examples of **doers. Type two** managers are analyzers and problem-solvers. These people are skilled in handling figures. They are engineers, accountants, and systems analysts.

A primary emphasis of business schools, said Leavitt, has been on producing Type two managers, analyzers, and problem-solvers with a penchant for numbers, and a secondary emphasis has been on producing Type three managers, the people-people, but business schools have had almost no concern with creating Type one managers, who are what companies need most. **Type one** managers see what might be; they have visions of a different future and, despite uncertainty and risk, they are able to lead others in its pursuit.

Many of the managers whom I sampled held MBA degrees, and most of them acted courageously. But, in support of Leavitt's observations, it is the case that of those managers who claimed never to have acted courageously a slightly disproportionate share were MBA graduates.

In the light of these observations and data, we are faced with the unwelcome possibility that, despite its many benefits, some common forms of management education may be converting managers into followers who are servants of a rational God. The religion that they promulgate places unquestioned faith in numbers and their analysis, events external to self. Such a religion places a premium on appearing cool, rational, and methodical. Passionate, courageous acts are out of keeping with its basic tenets. These followers piously crunch numbers, quantify, and analyze. They are often skilled at making presentations using charts, and more charts, and still more charts, but suffer some panic when required to make decisions in the absence of foolproof data or precise guidelines; freeze when given responsibility for people and profit; and hunker down when the only thing that will take an organization forward is courageous action.

When managers hunker down, the natural drift toward ideacide moves more swiftly. Organizations that place special emphasis on hierarchy or on harmony, those which deliberately or inadvertently design reward structures that create followers and punish leaders, and those that embrace an irrational faith in rationality, have all been identified as places where ideacide grows, eventually stifling courageous initiative. One other recurrent, unavoidable organizational circumstance joins these four, and stands condemned as a primary cause of ideacide. Unlike the first four culprits, which are of an organization's own making, this one is external and is imposed on organizations, always against their wishes. I am speaking of crisis and the individual stress that it produces.

Organizations that, all at once, find themselves going belly-up because of declining profits caused by increasing costs, tougher competitors, stiffer regulations or shrinking markets, have a great need for new ideas and creative problem solving. Unfortunately, the same disturbing organizational conditions that produce this need also produce stress in men and women in the organization. With stress people often do what comes naturally, and the behavior and thinking that tends to come naturally to people when they are stressed, paradoxically, blocks access to the courageously innovative ideas which are so desperately needed. That is exactly what happened in the mid-1970s when, my data show, the American business community suffered an eight-year famine in managerial courage.

Chapter Five

Organizational Crisis and Ideacide: Eight Years of Famine

"An Organizational Pathology Endangers National Recovery"

Three hundred years before the famine began, forces were already transforming human communities in ways that ultimately caused individual initiative and courage to become trademarks of American character. Before that time institutional authority was commonly vested in elites by force, tradition, religious sanction, magic, and the birthright of succession. Popular mandate was uncommon in human affairs, and individuals were ruled by authorities whom they rarely had the right to choose. Theirs was a world of obligations, not rights; duties, not initiative; and obedience, not courage. Although the seeds of change were already sown, for example, the Greek city states and the Magna Carta, it was not until the seventeenth and eighteenth centuries that fundamental changes in the relationship between individuals and authorities occurred. James MacGregor Burns comments:

> Spreading through Europe and America, powerful new doctrines proclaimed the rights of individuals against rulers, set forth goals and values beyond those of simply order and security, and called for liberty, equality, fraternity, and even the pursuit of happiness.

Nowhere was the call heard more clearly than in the new American nation where, more than being simply safeguarded against the whims of tyrannical rulers, individuals were themselves invested with the power of authority. The exercise of free choice in determining the course of their personal lives was limited by neither legal constraint nor tradition; and, as a consequence of constitutional mandate and emerging tradition, they possessed the right to periodically join with others in order to determine which authority would temporarily act as custodian of their community's affairs. Clearly, the sociopolitical conditions shaping American self-concept were different from those experienced by the shackled societies of earlier times.

I am not claiming that their sociopolitical experience, or any other one experience, single-handedly shaped the American character. It is simply that this experience, then unique to world history, synthesizes the kind of forces which were at work. Henry Steele Commager concludes that

> It was not, in short, particular environments that determined the American character or created the American type, but the whole of the American environment—the sense of spaciousness, the invitation to mobility, the atmosphere of independence, the encouragement to enterprise and to optimism.

Although all of the specific causes cannot be neatly identified and packaged for orderly display, it is clear that something novel occurred with the birth of the United States. It was witnessed at the time by that remarkably astute observer of America, Alexis de Tocqueville. De Tocqueville offered history with an astonishing comparison when he described what was occurring in the infant nation: "The people reign in the American political world as the Deity does in the universe. They are the cause and aim of all things; everything comes from them, and everything is absorbed in them." Wearing neither cross nor crown, the individual citizen prevailed.

Underneath all, individuals
I swear nothing is good to me now that ignores individuals,
The American compact is altogether with individuals,
The only government is that which makes minute of
*   individuals*

By Blue Ontario's Shore*
WALT WHITMAN

Whitman's passion echoes America's character and cultural commitments.

For a time, America's experience in war and peace served only to reinforce what was already there. Looking back from the vantage point of the mid-twentieth century, Commager began his book *The American Mind* with the following thoughts: "Over a period of two and a half centuries, marked by such adventures as few other people had known, Americans had created an American character and formulated an American Philosophy." The character and the philosophy, he said, elude easy definition, ". . . yet both were unmistakable. Certainly the hundreds of foreign visitors who swarmed over America and embarked so glibly upon interpretation had no difficulty in distinguishing American from Old World character. . . ."

*Reprinted by permission of New York University Press from WALT WHITMAN: LEAVES OF GRASS, READER'S COMPREHENSIVE EDITION, edited by Harold W. Blodgett and Sculley Bradley. Copyright © 1965 by New York University.

In their armed rebellion, as well as in their law, manner, story, and song, Americans rejected the Old World and its traditions, especially its reliance on social pedigree as a basis for establishing inequalities among people. The consequence for American character, and particularly for the role of individual initiative and courage in American culture, was almost without parallel. American heroes were not heirs, they were self-made people, individuals from common social background, diamonds in the rough who climbed from poverty into plenty through individual initiative, risk taking, and courage. America provided the Protestant ethic with fresh meaning: Individual glory, success, and achievement resulted from one's own efforts, from hard work, thrift, and competitive struggle. A Horatio Alger story may be truly more a symbol of the American cultural dream than a real portrayal of most Americans' experiences, but that is just the point: It is a symbol, and in that symbol nestles the dreams of America: Society is imagined to be dynamic and open; anyone who dares can seek a path leading to the top. All that is required is hard work, initiative, and courage.

The American character shaped and, in turn, was shaped by the principle that a great equality exists among individuals. No one is legally entitled to succeed because of birth, education, or wealth. This sense of equality is more than economic and political. De Tocqueville, Commager, and other observers of America saw its spillover into social affairs, noting that it substitutes casual informality for traditional formality. Geoffrey Gorer, Englishman, world-renowned anthropologist, and author of *The American People*, a classic study of the American nation and its social patterns, remarks with surprise that bosses and subordinates call each other by Christian names. For most Americans it would be a surprise and probably an insult if someone responded to one's use of their first name by saying, "When you address me, please say Mr. (or Ms.)" That request presumes social superiority, and individual Americans have no social superiors, not in the Old World sense. Education, speech, achievement, family heritage, and wealth confer no interpersonal privilege. They do not create a class of people who are "one's betters." American social equality made it easier to confront, to "say your piece," and be courageous. The image in the American dream is not of a prince who provides for and presides over diffident, obedient subjects; it is of a town meeting where peers gather in order to confront and solve problems.

And how does authority fare under these conditions? Not as it did in the Old World, is the simple answer. Gorer observed that American attitudes toward authority have remained substantially unchanged since the framing of the American Constitution: authority is considered to be inherently bad and potentially dangerous. Americans are too practical not to realize that someone must be boss, but when that authority is loaned, curbs on its scope and magnitude must be legally assured, and those who hold such positions must be watched. Americans are not a people who hold authorities in awe, as if they were an inevitable font of wisdom or benevolence.

Commager says:

> The American's attitude toward authority, rules and regulations was the despair of bureaucrats and disciplinarians. Nowhere did he differ more sharply from his English cousins than in his attitude toward rule, for where the Englishman regarded the observance of rules as a positive pleasure, to the American a rule was at once an affront and a challenge. . . . Rules represented tradition, and discipline authority; he knew that his country had become great by flouting both and that in a land where everything was yet to be done and where the future was in his hands, he could continue to flout both with impunity.

Courageous dissent, daring to do differently, challenging established practice, were accepted as indispensable elements of America's and Americans' successes.

Stories, songs, and history lessons still romanticize the image of a courageous nobody, successfully challenging the authority of established practice. Americans love the plot, cherish the character, and desire to play the part. It's the American way.

In the same way as they confronted established practice, Americans related to the past by challenging its value for the future. Even today we see symptoms of this posture: Typically, the aged are not prized as guiding sages in contemporary America. As much as their treatment may be lamented, they are regularly set aside, ignored, dismissed, embarrassed, challenged, and laughed at because their ways are presumably old, and America is a nation seeking the new. It's the American way.

Americans have traditionally seen change as good. History for Americans is a progressive force and the future, not the past, has dominated their thinking. A nostalgically longed-for **golden time** never gleamed brightly enough to attract a backward glance. America looks forward, convinced that the best is yet to come, and individual initiative and courage are the keys to unlocking the door to that inevitably brighter tomorrow. M.I.T. professor Edgar Schein says that Americans possess a **proactive optimism,** that is, they believe that anything, including you and me, can be fixed through knowledge and technology—American know-how. Therefore, individuals need not accept their fate. If they make the effort, tomorrow will be better. It's the American way.

Powered by these cultural assumptions, Americans swaggered across the frontier and into the twentieth century, creating novel solutions to old problems, reinforcing the idea that tradition, established practice, and SOP were anchors to a lesser past, not propellants into a **golden future.**

"Nothing in all history had ever succeeded like America, and every American knew it," says Commager. "Collectively he had never known defeat, grinding poverty, or oppression, and he thought these misfortunes peculiar to the Old World." Progress, growth, expansion, and achievement were more than goals to be pursued, they **were** America's destiny. Confidence and optimism fueled effort. Nothing was out of reach. Americans firmly believed that it was their fate to succeed, yet they never became fatalistic. In order to share in the destiny of the collective, one had to work. If you failed, then it was because you neglected the opportunity. Events as recent as World War II fed American optimism, confidence, and feeling of invulnerability. Then, less than 30 years later, these precious cultural assumptions were shattered. Americans lost what seemed assured as their rightful place in the world. The impossible had occurred: Americans were vulnerable. Business, indeed the entire economy, had been brought to its knees by "foreigners." The presidency had been compromised. American armed forces failed to win a war. Stagflation set on the nation with a vengeance. Culturally inculcated beliefs, nay, self-evident truths held with unconscious fervor, were swiftly stamped "**invalid.**" American know-how, guts, the American way, had failed. The nation was wretched.

On October 31, 1975, the Committee on the Budget of the United States Senate, concerned about these upsetting events, convened a seminar on "consumer confidence and federal economic policy." It is easy to summarize the diagnostic conclusion of that seminar. Nationally renowned political advisor Pat Caddell, one of the experts who was asked to testify, did it for us when he said:

> In the 1950s and 1960s, people in general were very optimistic about the future of the country, even at a

time when the economy might be declining. Their
general feeling was that the country was on a very
strong upward move. Today was better than yesterday, tomorrow would be better than today.

But, he concluded, in 1973 that pattern showed a sharp
alteration. A great majority of Americans now believed
that the country was in decline and they shared "a great
hesitation and caution about where we are going in the
future."

The fact is that the index of consumer sentiment suffered serious decline in 1973–1974, and it would not
again reach pre-1973 levels until the early 1980s. Looking
at the index's depressing behavior in 1975, an insightful
scientist from the University of Michigan's Survey Research Center, Jay Schmeideskamp, wrote:

> It may take time to reverse the present deeply unfa-
> vorable attitude, especially the lack of confidence in
> government and in the economy. In both respects,
> current attitudes are sharply at variance with attitudes
> held during the last quarter century [This fellow was
> being scientifically conservative, speaking only about
> a period of time during which polls could document
> the claim], when most consumers considered pros-
> perity to be the normal condition and trusted the gov-
> ernment.

The pessimism exhibited by consumers was not out
of touch with reality. The industrial world's real economic growth averaged 6.1% in 1973; it fell to .7% in

1974 and turned negative in 1975. Interest rates swung in the double-digit direction. Output per worker hour averaged 3.3% growth each year from 1947 to 1973, then it dropped to .4%. In 1983 *New York Times* reporter Leonard Silk looked back at that troubled time and wrote, "The oil price explosion and the Arab oil embargo of 1973–74 dealt an unprecedented and lasting shock to the world economy, a shock that paradoxically brought both inflation and recession." In the same article James R. Schlesinger, former Secretary of Energy and an advisor at Lehman Brothers, Kuhn, Loeb, Inc., was quoted as saying, "From the standpoint of the 21st century, the year 1973 will stand out as marking a watershed." He said that the radical change in oil price at that time marks a separation between the "postwar era of unparalleled economic expansion" and the present era with its "unexpected economic difficulties."

But the series of hammer blows that the American people suffered at that time produced a shock that was more than economic, and the effects were more than financial. These events disrupted the psychological stability of the nation's business institutions, producing an "organizational pathology" that continues to endanger national industrial recovery. The Silk article touches on the heart of the matter when it discusses some observations by Walter Salant, a senior fellow at the Brookings Institution. Salant mentioned that times such as these place a premium on organizational adaptability and change. As we have seen, both those organizational processes require a challenge to established practice and a

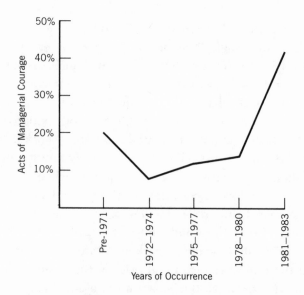

Figure 1. Years of occurrence—acts of managerial courage.

willingness to do things differently. Unfortunately, that is exactly what did *not* happen.

Apparently terrified of the unfamiliar, bewildering economic circumstances in which they found themselves, American management sought refuge by preserving what once was. New ideas were not forthcoming. Managerial conservatism blossomed, ideacide increased, and American business organizations suffered an eight-year famine of individual courage at the very time when it was most needed.

A simple plotting of the year in which managers reported acting courageously tells the story (see Figure 1). The earliest act of managerial courage reported in my questionnaires occurred in 1967, the most recent in 1983, but the occurrence of managerial courage was not evenly distributed across the intervening years (see Figure 1). The percentage of courageous acts that managers reported dipped dramatically sometime in that fateful period between 1972 and 1974 and did not fully recover for eight years. Is it a mere coincidence that the drop coincides with events that pummeled the American dream? I doubt it. Between 1972 and 1974 the illusion of American economic primacy was smashed. An unquestioned destiny was denied. A sense of vulnerability replaced a conviction of invincibility. Americans were suddenly uncertain of their unconquerability. For the first time, perhaps, there was a national sense of defeat. Americans hunkered down self-protectively. They longed for a past that had mysteriously vanished. They feared a future that was unknown. Corporate caretakers behaved in the most human of ways. Wanting to preserve what remained of what was, they embraced the status quo and, in so doing, paradoxically endangered the very thing that they wanted restored, American corporate success.

It was 1975 and our costs were skyrocketing. Budgeting and planning were jokes. I mean you couldn't predict what vendors were going to do next month, much less next year. They were under the same pressure from their suppliers. The common wisdom was to cut back staff, curtail or eliminate weak product lines, reduce R&D, trim all the extras—training, employee relations, security—or put them out under contract. New product marketing—forget it, everyone said

"No! Too expensive, too risky, not in this climate, go with what works." It seemed to me that everyone was working hard, but at the wrong things. It was old wine, stale old wine. We needed some things that were fresh, new, and bubbling.

I felt it was wrong. We had to have new business options. No one wanted to hear what I had to say and believe me I said it everywhere—at every meeting. I just couldn't convince people to try. What they wanted—and it made some sense—was to move with what they were most certain about. Everything was being tightened and centralized: Limits of authority, other cost controls, purchasing decisions. Everything.

I tried to get my boss to agree to let me present a plan that had to do with a complicated arrangement for resourcing and producing certain items to our senior group. He was very reluctant. Finally he agreed but set it up in a way that left him out—you know, so that he wouldn't be responsible for me. He was only doing what he needed to, to stay safe. I can't blame him in that climate, but it left me very exposed, if you know what I mean.

The presentation was something of a disaster. They were all over me: "How much will it cost?" "How quickly will you return capital invested?" "Where has it been tried?" I knew that here was a group of frightened people. I couldn't stay. That was not a place where I could see myself. Probably it was the best thing that happened. Within a year I set up my own business using some of the ideas that they never really heard. It's ironic. I mean how your life turns. If they

hadn't been so scared, I'd probably still be there. I
guess I've got the Arabs to thank for my career.

The plastics firm owned by the 35-year-old CEO who
was speaking to me grossed nearly $6.5 million in 1982,
when we had this conversation. Seven years earlier,
when so many managers hunkered down in order to protect themselves from the crisis that engulfed American
business, he was one of the few who dared. Sadly, the fate
that awaited his ideas within his former organization was
not an uncommon one for ideas, courageously offered,
during those stressful years of the mid-1970s. Other data
tell us that the decrease of courageous initiative in that
period was accompanied by a rise in ideacide. Let's look
at the probability with which acts of managerial courage
met with success during this past decade and one-half. It
has changed, and the pattern of change seems almost certainly a reflection of national and world events.

American business does not operate in splendid isolation. Its treatment of managers and their acts of courage—so critical to organizational regeneration—are both
shaped by the socioeconomic milieu within which the
business operates. Historical time and place seem as if
they should be remote influences on the course and consequence of acts of managerial courage, but they are not.
All behavior, including acts of managerial courage, is
seen through a lens which is colored by time and place.
On occasion, an act's qualities are distorted as the lens
blurs our sight. As is the case with the metaphorical gold-
fish in the bowl, who is unaware of the surrounding wa-

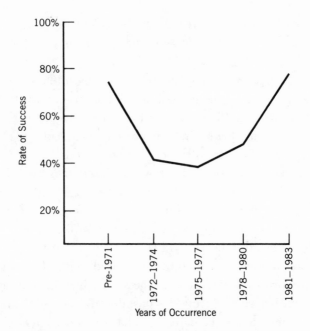

Figure 2. Years of occurrence—rate of success.

ter, the power of these remote influences eludes our conscious experience. But the effect is there nonetheless, and it can be shocking when brought into awareness. I was shocked the moment I observed modern history's effect on the success and failure of acts of managerial courage.

Here in Figure 2 we have evidence of what I believe can be labeled a **sociogenic** effect on managerial behavior in organizations. Seemingly distant societal events permeated organizational walls, altering the likelihood that an act of managerial courage escaped ideacide. And the

· 132 ·

evidence of sociogenic effects does not stop here. If we turn over the coin and look at the behavior of managers who acted courageously, we also see sociogenic processes at work. In this case, the issues that courageous managers challenged reflect the historical period and seem not to be a simple, objective consequence of self-contained organizational matters.

Overall, the issues that managers elected to challenge were divided into four categories:

1. Matters of business
2. Matters concerning the behavior of superiors
3. Matters concerning the behavior of subordinates
4. Matters concerning ethical principle

In total, 58% of courageous acts dealt with business issues, 27% with the behavior of superiors, 4% with the behavior of subordinates, and 11% with ethical principle.

There is a clear indication, however, that superiors' behavior became more of an issue between 1972 and 1974 than it previously had been or would be during the next decade. Remembering the Vietnam War, Watergate, and the documented rise of public mistrust in authorities, the pattern seems more than a coincidence. Of the managers' courageous acts between 1972 and 1974, 46% were concerned with superiors' behavior. That is up from the 32% figure in the pre-1971 period, and considerably above the 7, 22, and 29% totals that we find in the 1975–1977, 1978–1980, and 1981–1983 periods, respectively.

The tragic years between 1972 and 1974 were also a

time when courageous acts involving business issues reached a comparative low. Only 36% of the acts during that period focused on business matters, compared with 41% in the pre-1971 period, and 79% in 1975–1977, 67% in 1978–1980, and 62% in 1981–1983. (We must remember that although the 1973 oil embargo may have put the nail in the coffin, the pre-1971 period was also a time of war in Vietnam, assassinations, civil rights unrest, and university upheaval. From this perspective, the comparative similarity between the pre-1971 data and those from the 1972–1974 period make sense.)

Finally, courageous acts involving ethical issues reach their peak of 18% in those turbulent Vietnam/Watergate days prior to 1974. The percentage falls to 14% for the 1975–1977 period and to zero in 1978–1980. Most recently, between 1981–1983, it has risen to just under 9% of the total. (No differences in the percentage of courageous acts focusing on subordinate behavior were at all evident.) These patterns support the interpretations of sociogenic effects that I made earlier: The frequency of individual acts of managerial courage, their focus, and their success all seem to have been affected by economic, social, and political crises which began outside organizational walls.

By 1974 America had experienced a historical dislocation. The nation's continuity with its psychological past was fractured. The cultural myths which supported and shaped American character lost their validity and became targets of ridicule and mockery. The stress induced by the rapid, undesirable change caused managers to behave in two different maladaptive ways, by **flighting** and by **fighting.** First, many American businesspeople broke and ran. They were disillusioned, bewildered, frightened, and their first response was to take flight from reality by doing more of what they had been doing, acting as if nothing had changed.

Business Week magazine in its February 13, 1984, issue comments, "The flow of innovation, as measured by such indicators as patents issued per year, began to shrink drastically in the 1970s and economists worried that the U.S. was losing its inventiveness." It would be bold, but foolish, to assert that this occurred only because courage declined. Technological innovation reflects prior R&D expenditures and other nonpsychological business considerations. Even so, it would be wrong to completely dismiss the possibility that this decline also both reflected and reinforced the timid, backpedaling managerial mentality of the early 1970s. Courageous business initiatives, bold challenges of the suddenly inadequate existing policies and strategies plummeted in that period. Responding as people commonly do to crisis, in organizations and elsewhere, one group of managers took flight from the altered reality by pretending nothing had happened. They stood still, trying not to worsen the boat's already tumultuous rocking. Only, the world had changed and one could not safely stand still. Courageous challenge of established business practice was desperately needed, but tragically absent.

Instead of taking flight in response to the crisis, a second group of managers behaved maladaptively by starting a fight. But the fight that they started seems to be more a reflection of their concerns about events outside the organization than it was a response to organizational needs. This maladaptive fight response is reflected in the choice of issues that these courageous managers challenged. Shifting from their traditional focus on business matters, in and around the crucial period from 1972–1974, many managers were acting as if they chose to fight broader societal battles in the microcosm of the larger society that corporate life is. Challenges to superior behavior and matters of ethical principle both reached their zeniths in those years of disappointment and disillusionment with authorities and institutions. (I hasten to note that these changes of focus do **not** reflect the activity of any single age group.) One retired manager whom I met in 1984 told me the following story:

> There was this one group of folks I remember back about 9, no 10 years ago, in the spring of 1974 it was, just before the Nixon resignation, I'm sure. You couldn't really say just who they were, in the sense that they were all different and such. Mostly young, but several older folks. Good workers. Maybe one or two lazy types.
>
> They were real upset about how we were doing business, using our profits. We didn't do defense work then, never have actually, but we were, are, a for-profit company. They wanted us to use funds for—I forget the details, but, you know, housing, education—like training minorities. Things of that sort.

Business does have its responsibilities—I really don't object to the basic idea. You've just got to think about where you draw the line. Just what **is** your responsibility isn't all that clear now, is it? These folks just didn't have a sense of perspective. They were too "caught up," might be the way to say it. We weren't the United States government.

Perhaps I'm being a bit harsh. Sometimes people have no other place to speak about what's ailing them. It was the times. They were troubled times.

Other times and other newsmaking events would likely have a different, perhaps even a positive, effect on organization life. War and natural calamity, for example, might very well produce a greater concern with business issues and a willingness to explore ideas that depart from the current consensus. But the early 1970s had their own brand of trouble and it had special consequences for organizations.

Ultimately, the stressful sociogenic intrusion of that period into corporate life produced an organizational pathology whereby the system was denied the very individual managerial behavior which was most needed to rescue it from its malady and stimulate organizational regeneration.

That tragically ironic consequence is a potential pitfall for any organization in crisis. Without care and special attention, the individual human stress which accompanies difficult times in organization life is clearly capable of causing an unhealthy constriction of courageous initiative. Curbing ideacide requires tough, hard managerial work. Such effort must become a priority for managers. Some practical means of achieving that goal are discussed in later chapters. For the moment, however, I believe that there is benefit in examining other matters which bear on developing essential diagnostic insight into the problem of ideacide and the role of managerial courage in contemporary corporate life.

By the late 1970s and early 1980s, the flight–fight pattern of the crisis years was changing. The change was paralleled by movement in the index of consumer sentiment and also by events in what George Gilder, author of *The Spirit of Enterprise,* calls the "entrepreneurial economy." Gilder says:

> After the capital gains tax cut of 1978, all the indices of the entrepreneurial economy moved massively up, as a long backlog of innovations at last found significant funding. By the end of the year, new commitments to venture capital funds had risen almost fifteen-fold, from $39 million in 1977, to $570 million in 1978.

The progress continued steadily so that "by the end of 1983 the pot of venture funds soared to $11.5 billion [and] . . . the number of major venture capital partnerships soared . . . from 25 in 1973 to over 200 ten years later." In other business-related arenas there were echoes of these events: The number of new stock issues rose 60% between 1978 and 1980, and the total capital raised in new public issues went from $300 million in the mid-

1970s to $13 billion in 1983. A national recovery was beginning and courage was on the upswing.

Am I unnecessarily pessimistic? Perhaps. But I feel no relief, nor do I rest easy, because the frequency of managerial courage seems to have risen to a point beyond the pre-1971 level. I see no reason to proclaim that the crisis is over, the organizational pathology remedied. There are subtleties in the data which suggest that the restoration of managerial courage in organizations is tenuous and that organization regeneration remains in danger. I note that (1) the trend line of courageous acts which focus on superiors' behavior is upward; (2) the trend line of acts concerned with matters of ethics is also upward; and while these alone are not cause for alarm, (3) the trend line of courageous acts concerned with business matters has tilted downward. I also note that nearly half (46%) of the managers who spoke with me in 1983 felt that managerial courage was declining. Fewer (29%) believed that it was increasing, and fewer still (25%) thought it was at a standstill. This, despite the fact that 86% of these managers felt that organizations would benefit from **more** instances of managerial courage.

Three major reasons for the current decline in managerial courage were offered: (1) **The economy** was sour and unpredictable, causing higher unemployment and corporate belt tightening and making a manager's current job more dear. The potential costs for courageous acts are too great under these conditions; (2) Changing **management styles** through the 1970s and early 1980s were stifling managerial courage. Unsurprisingly, two opposite management styles were identified as having this chilling effect. One style placed excessive emphasis on maintaining a strong, bureaucratic hierarchy, and the second placed excessive emphasis on maintaining harmony and consensual decision making. And (3) Managers who answered my questions said that **The new generation** managers had ideals and aspirations which made them less loyal, involved, or caring insofar as the company was concerned. They valued their own security and material well-being, but not corporate success. "Managers like that," I was told, "don't take risks. Matter of fact, they probably can't imagine why anyone would be courageous when the only one to benefit was the organization."

Recent studies of the values and attitudes of new entrants into organization life confirm the observations of these managers. In an article titled "Loyal to What?" Kevin McDermott, compares personnel who were first-level managers at ATT in the past few years with a like group of managers who occupied the same positions during the mid-fifties. The new generation of managers was less committed to climbing the organizational ladder. To me, the data describe a group that is much more concerned with getting along than with getting ahead. In an article concerned with these very issues entitled, "The New Organization Man," the author, John Thackray says that Daniel Yankelovich, the famous public opinion pollster, reports data suggesting that the new generation's values are more hedonistic and self-centered. If this were all that could be said about the personal profile of the new generation of managers, then we might give up in total despair, for it is certainly not the stuff of courage. Managerial courage requires a commitment to something outside of oneself. It requires a concern for an organization's growth and success.

Fortunately, more can be said. Oddly enough, the smaller percentage of managers who felt that managerial courage was increasing said that the principal reason for the increase was, of all things, **the new generation**! What they said of these people was:

> The younger generation of managers is more outspoken. They're not so fearful about losing their positions. They're more self-confident.

> We see a new generation of younger, short-service managers, with less fear of authority, replacing the long-service (single company career) generation.

> The young, new generation of managers' values encourage speaking out, asking "why?" The new generation of managers have greater professional integrity and independence.

> Sociocultural changes have caused the new generation to be more creative, less narrow-minded.

These observations offer hope that the legacy of the 1970s is not totally negative. As a result of their experiences during the last decade, some **new generation** managers may have acquired personal qualities which enhance the likelihood that they will engage in acts of managerial courage. Perhaps these are the people that

Admiral Hyman G. Rickover (U.S.N. Ret.) was referring to when he advised us that:

> Subordinates are needed who are committed to goals rather than to process and who are not afraid to criticize when they no longer agree with the goals. . . . What is required is someone to disturb the self-assurance of a staff. Someone who will say: "We are getting into a mess"!

It is fashionable nowadays to attack "brute integrity" and "rugged individualism" in corporate life, claiming that it is a negative part of American management's cultural endowment. The critics point to images of John Wayne managing a crisis by swaggering up a street and shooting it out—bluntly, arrogantly, without regard for others. In corporate life, the "tell it like it is" translation of this image of masculinity, say the critics, causes pain and produces destructive relationships. Harold Geneen, some people's **bête noire,** is often portrayed as the epitome of this kind of tough, rugged manager, a kind of cowboy capitalist. In their enthusiasm the critics forget that integrity does not need to be **brute** and individualism does not need to be **rugged.** Their stereotypic view is that lack of compassion and egocentric insensitivity are invariably characteristic of leaders who are capable of making decisions on their own, even in opposition to majority desires. This false idea has taken a firm hold on many managers and scholars, causing an overzealous and uncritical acceptance of several alternative management styles, the most recent one being a Japanese import.

Chapter Six

The Japanese Paradox

"Crossing in a Group. It's Not Scary."

If there were a "business IQ" test, then one question might be: What do each of the following have in common? **Toyota, Panasonic, Canon, Sony, Datsun (Nissan), Suzuki, Quasar, Mazda, Nikon, Honda, Minolta, Seiko, Sanyo, Toshiba, and Yamaha.** On this imaginary IQ test some credit would have to be given for at least two related answers: First, all of these are familiar brand names; and second, for that very reason, all of these names are evidence of Japan's spectacular business success. Advancing beyond its flimsy, knick-knack products of crepe paper, cardboard, and straw, sometime during the past two or three decades Japan adapted the technical, managerial, and marketing know-how of American and European firms, and the nation was reborn as the world's preeminent industrial society. Competitors watched, with seeming helplessness, as their products were bypassed by consumers who were eagerly grabbing for quality items, reassuringly labeled, "Made in Japan."

Now, with its gains in a wide range of markets apparently secure, Japan, Inc. is launching a fresh assault on high technology industries like computers, semiconductors, and bioengineering. Some believe that by faithfully mimicking Japanese managerial practices other industrial nations can recapture lost ground and defend themselves against newly planned incursions. The idea is wrong. It reflects a misunderstanding of the Japanese and what they have done.

For me, an exaggerated but not unwarranted image of Japan and Japanese management is captured by a comic Japanese young people's poem:

Red light.
Crossing in a group
It's not scary.

What it says is that, for individual Japanese, security comes from being part of a group (humorously, even when the danger might be an onrushing truck) and not from independent initiative.

Once, while riding the bullet train leaving Tokyo, I was chatting with a Japanese manager with whom I had worked, about differences in the self-images of American and Japanese workers. "Americans," he said to me as the orderly, crowded countryside noiselessly sped by at more than 100 miles per hour, "say 'I'm OK—you're OK,' but in Japan we say 'We're OK—I'm OK.'" I understand the distinction that he was making. It is evident when you work with Japanese and frequently cited in most scholarly comparisons of America and Japan: Japanese culture encourages the expression of self-identity through group membership. Individual worth, therefore, is in large measure a derivative of group achievement and one's contribution to it. In the United States, however, individual initiative and achievement are commonly identified as the most culturally consistent ways of expressing self-identity. Individual worth is a product of one's own accomplishments.

Japanese tend to view this sort of individualistic orientation in life's affairs as "selfish" and "inconsiderate." It runs counter to the central tendency of their culture which is infused with the Confucianist idea that human perfectibility is attainable through service to family and community. Self-development, for the Japanese, happens when one pursues the highest standards of service for others, rather than personal gain or prominence. There is, for them, special virtue in fulfilling one's duty and responsibility to the group. In the not-too-distant past, the group was the rice-growing community and the feudal clan; nowadays it is the organization.

The central tenets of the cultural assumptions guiding Japanese life provide an evident and indisputable contrast to a Western ethos which places greater emphasis on the redemptive virtue of individual action and achievement. The Western idea allows for and encourages mavericks who try to "do it their way," who do not bow before tradition but challenge it, emboldened by a presumption of institutional and, even, parental fallibility. "Japan's Synergistic Society," an article written by Robert R. Rehder and published in a 1981 issue of the *Management Review*, identifies at least one reason why Japan is not a hospitable breeding ground for mavericks. Rehder says that the society works because "the cultural value system of subordination of self to higher collective goals combines with a homogeneous population's need to achieve and a broad belief in work as the highest self-fulfillment goal." Mavericks flourish in cultures that extoll individual independence, not in those that endorse subordination of self.

"Crossing in a group. It's not scary," signals the psychological comfort that the Japanese experience when they are immersed in a group. Apropos of this, in 1984 the American Psychological Association's journal, the *American Psychologist*, published an article by professors John Weisz, Fred Rothbaum and Thomas Blackburn, which was concerned with the "psychology of control in America and Japan." It noted that a popular Japanese slogan is, "Your team can win, even if you cannot." The authors of this article point out that scholars, "see in this slogan a traditional Japanese ethical principle: The worker dedicates self to the advancement of the group, and in this way he manages to achieve a kind of mystical union with his group." The preeminence of the work group in a Japanese's life is, in a small way, evident in the findings of A.M. Whitehall, published in a 1964 issue of the reputable *Journal of Applied Psychology*. The study showed that 66% of Japanese workers rated their companies **and** their personal lives as being **at least equal** to one another in importance, but only 24% of the American workers sampled said that they felt the same way; many more felt that personal life was more important.

Unsurprisingly, Japanese workers will go to great lengths in order to preserve the harmony of this union between the individual and the work group. The guiding concept they call **Wa,** or harmony among group members. In a paper entitled "Emerging trends of human resources management in Japan," presented to the International Conference on Human Resources Management, which met in Manila in 1982, Seiji Yamamoto, a Japanese human resources specialist, said that **Wa** encourages Japanese employees to (1) be modest and humble, (2) deny self-interest, and (3) punish violations of these virtues.

Japanese organizations are molded from the stuff of Japanese society. Employees arrive filled with a sense of service to the whole, a capacity to be modest, humble, and subordinate to the *team,* and a commitment to maintaining group harmony. The mold produces forces which discourage employees from pursuing individual initiative which might cause friction, and encourages them to follow tradition by fulfilling their prescribed duties and responsibilities. They are pressured to **move with the group** and stick together in what the Japanese call a **natto** society. What is **natto**? It is a thick, almost glue like, fermented soy bean paste that is rich with nutrition—a fitting symbol for the Japanese organizational processes that we are discussing. In return for their employees sticking together, loyalty, and conformity, and no doubt as a means of maintaining it, Japanese companies typically provide their employees with what many Western observers regard as an unusual degree of nurturance.

This nurturance goes beyond the ordinary and often alluded-to business welfarism that is so characteristic of Japan. The welfarism is exemplified by company sponsored housing, recreation, health care, and consumer co-ops. But, in reality, these are mere symbols of something much more profound. Japanese companies are also providing employees with a sense of belonging, of being part of a benevolent group that will attend to its members' interests. This social/psychological embrace—the mystical union that was mentioned before—more than the objective, tangible benefits of business welfarism, is what maintains the Japanese loyalty and commitment.

When Japanese managers were asked, "Why did you behave as you did?," 62% said that they acted courageously because they felt that they were a "unique resource that the organization could not do without." When American managers were asked the same question, in a total reversal of the pattern 80% said that being a unique resource had **nothing** at all to do with their behavior. The odd part is that in objective terms, if jobs are examined, the Japanese managers who answered the question do not appear to be very different from managers in the American sample. No great number were professionals with special talents, nor were they scientists with rare skill. In fact there were even fewer of these types than in the American sample. If you want to understand what was happening here, forget an objective, rational explanation. The key to understanding this finding is to recognize that the **natto** society causes the Japanese to feel important, wanted, and even indispensable. They are part of a family.

Kohei Goshi, Chairman of the Japan Productivity Center, addressed this issue at a seminar on Japanese personnel management and industrial practice which met in Singapore during 1981. He was quoted in a newspaper article, "Cooperation Is the Key to Productivity," which appeared in *The Straits Times* (a local newspaper), as saying that in order to keep employees loyal and committed, Japanese organizations create "a consciousness of seeing the company as an extention of the family." In a book that is used to orient employees at **TDK** Electronics, one of Japan's more successful companies, the president, Sono Fukujiro, is explicit in his advocacy of this familial image in corporate life. He says, "I urge you, as heads of departments and sections, to regard those in your charge as your own children and educate them to be children you can be proud of." At other points in the book he admonishes and advises employees with all the presumption of a loving father:

> If you don't already do so, I would ask employees to make sure you greet your families properly every morning and to make sure you give all the other appropriate greetings, such as those before meals, when leaving the house, and on returning here.

> Now that I've read employees' comments on the history of **TDK**, I must say young people today are poor at expressing themselves. Their compositions are immature and lacking in thought, not to mention misspellings and careless omissions of words. This must be from too much television and not reading enough. You're earning decent salaries and you've reached an age when you should be reinvesting in yourselves. I strongly suggest, therefore, that you make a point of reading books.

The familiar claim, "A family that prays together, stays together," reflects the broader idea that ritual can be used to strengthen bonds among group members. The lesson is not lost in Japan where the use of ritual in organization life is comparatively common. For example, there are approximately 80,000 employees working for Matsushita in Japan and they all start their workday in the same way, by reciting the company objectives: "National service through industry, fairness, harmony and cooperation, struggle for betterment, courtesy and humility, adjustment and assimilation, and gratitude." When the recitation is completed, they sing the company song, "Love, light and dream," and then they begin their work.

What is the consequence of this daily group ritual? Well, Steve Lohr, who often writes about Japanese industry, tells us in his December, 1982, *New York Times* article "Matsushita: The Cautious Giant":

> Odd as it may seem to Westerners, there is a strong family-like bond in many Japanese companies, and a loyalty to the enterprise and to each other that seems to have the character of a religious devotion. Chief executives often talk to their responsibility for the spiritual well-being of their employees.

Support for Lohr's observation is evident in **TDK**'s orientation booklet where its president, Sono Fukujiro, writes:

> A company both creates and nurtures culture. The social responsibility of the company extends across a very wide range, from making products and merchandise of social value to satisfying the material and spiritual need of its employees.

Thus, Japanese organizations draw on culturally induced dispositions and create a social/psychological setting within which individual employees are more prone
to view themselves as group members than as individual
actors. From this perspective their individual accomplishments are subordinate to group success, and their
self-evaluations rest heavily on the degree to which they
fulfill prescribed duties and responsibilities in harmony
with other group members. The pressure to conform
being experienced by Japanese managers, therefore, is
less a product of overt and brutish hierarchical constraint
than it is the result of **peer group influence** and **culturally
induced dispositions** inculcated within the managers
themselves. Japanese management practices are structured in a fashion that both enhances and exploits these
pressures. Consequently, despite all the benefits so ably
and accurately described by others during the past few
years, the means of problem solving and decision making
in Japanese organizations must be regarded as a primary
contributor to, and exploiter of, the pressure to conform.

The Nippon Steel Corporation has a book, written in
both English and Japanese, that is titled *Nippon: The
Land and Its People.* In its foreword the book explains
that,

> Like many Japanese companies, Nippon Steel has
> been internationalizing its business operations very
> rapidly the past few years, with the result that the em-
> ployees are now coming into increasingly frequent
> contact with foreigners, both in Japan and overseas.

At such times, the conversation often turns to subjects about Japan, and our employees are often asked about Japanese culture and other aspects of their country. Many of these questions are extremely difficult to answer accurately and to the satisfaction of the inquirer. . . . This book is compiled to help eliminate these problems.

The collective character of Japanese problem solving and decision making is described on pages 113 and 114 of that book. I cannot efficiently improve on what is written there:

> The person in charge draws up the original plan in written form and obtains the approval of his seniors in ascending order: from supervisor to manager to general manager. The approval of officers in related departments is obtained before the final executive decision on the plan. In Japan, this process is called the **ringi** system.

In his book, *Iemoto: The Heart of Japan*, F. L. K. Hsu describes five components of the **ringi** system: (1) a written proposal is prepared by the responsible group; (2) with care for maintaining harmony, the proposal is informally and cautiously passed by people at the same level as the initiating group; (3) with the same care and caution, the proposal is informally shared up and down the hierarchy; (4) a final plan is prepared and formal approval(s) are designated by responsible individuals who affix their seals to the proposal document; and (5) in keeping with traditional modesty and humility, ambiguity about who was responsible for the proposal is deliberately maintained.

To Western eyes, **ringi** involves what seems like an endless series of meetings (called the **kaigi** system). About these meetings, the Nippon Steel Corporation's book says:

> Such meetings, with many people stating their opinions and making proposals, are not always so efficient; however, the advancing of various opinions leads to better decisions and, moreover, all those present have a feeling of having participated in the plans. This leads to a smoother implementation of the matter which has been decided on.

Arthur S. Golden, who speaks Japanese and worked for two years in Japan for a Japanese company, Matsushita, describes one of these meetings in a *New York Times* article called, "Group Think in Japan, Inc." His description makes it clear that at such a meeting individuals strive hard not to stand out by either confronting ideas or courageously dissenting from the group point of view.

Golden says that first a report is presented. The boss nods, and everyone provides modest support after showing proper humility. Then a thought, perhaps more properly described as an "afterthought," is offered by someone who immediately disowns it, claiming that it is only for consideration and not at all a refutation of what has been offered. The meeting normally proceeds in this way, without any one vigorously attacking or defending a proposal. Because of the process no one person is in a position to claim credit for the plan; no one person has taken a position which makes him prominent and, ultimately, the group, aided by culturally induced individual behaviors, emerges as the originator and owner of the final plan. The consequence of this entire Japanese system of decision making is paradoxical: it provides many physical opportunities for managers to behave courageously at the same time that it produces extraordinary group and internal pressure on them to conform.

Japanese managers in my sample, for example, believed that their organizations were providing opportunity for them to speak out. When they were asked about their organization's encouragement of courageous behavior, 77% said that their organizations encouraged it, in contrast to a mere 28% of American managers. This difference might lead one to suspect that Japanese superiors and subordinates provided managers with lots of support but it is not so. If we examine the way in which superiors in Japan **actually** dealt with acts of managerial courage, we find that the reality for Japanese managers is hardly different from that of American managers.

The behavior of immediate bosses of courageous Japanese managers was a near replica of their U.S. counterparts: 39% reputedly supported the managers' courageous acts and 61% were described as either not involved (15%) or opposed (46%). The pattern is almost, but not quite, the same for superiors other than immediate bosses: 31%, nearly the same proportions as in the U.S., were described as supporters of the managers' courageous acts but, following the Japanese tradition of a more remote, less hands-on senior management style, among those **not supporting** the courageous initiative, most (62%) were described as "not involved" and only 7% as directly opposed. (By contrast, in the United States, 48% of these higher-ups were seen as directly opposed.) As in the United States, Japanese subordinates tended to be seen as supporting their managers' courageous acts: 62% did so, and only 38% were either not involved (15%) or opposed (23%).

This pattern of parallel with the United States continues when we examine how support of others affected the likelihood of success and failure. Overall, 69% of courageous acts by Japanese managers succeeded and 31% failed. Hardly different from the American experience. Moreover, as in the United States, support of immediate bosses and higher-ups went a long way toward guaranteeing success (80% of those reporting support of immediate bosses and 100% of those reporting support from other higher-ups succeeded). Also, as in the United States, lack of support from superiors by no means guaranteed failure (about 60% of those reporting lack of support by higher-ups succeeded).

Further, in Japan, organizational responses to courageous managerial initiatives were affected by the support of others in pretty much the same way as it was in the United States—subordinate support helped some, but boss and higher-up support helped a lot: 12% of courageous Japanese managers who claimed subordinate support were treated negatively by the organization, but not a single Japanese manager who said that he or she had the backing of immediate bosses and other higher-ups experienced a negative outcome. Evidently, Japanese managers who want to act courageously need to get their alliances straight, just as American managers do.

Thus, in terms of actual support for courageous acts and the likelihood of success and failure, Japan does not appear to be very different from the United States. This is true despite the widespread sense by Japanese managers that their organizations encourage courageous managerial behavior. The strangest part is that although Japanese managers feel better than Americans about organizational support and, in fact, are no worse off than Americans in terms of actual support, they still are **much less likely** to behave courageously. They themselves say so. When asked about the frequency of courageous behavior in their organizations, for example, over 60% of Japanese managers in this sample said that fewer than 10% of managers in their organizations have acted courageously (that view is about twice as dismal as that held by U.S. managers) and 100%, my whole sample of Japanese managers, said that fewer than 40% of their fellows have acted courageously, which is about a 25% gloomier picture than the one painted by their American counterparts.

These subjective observations by Japanese managers are supported by more objective evidence: only 15% of the American managers said that they had never acted courageously during their careers and therefore couldn't

answer my questions, but more than twice that proportion, approximately 40% of the Japanese managers, said
that they had never done so. The relative absence of Japanese managerial courage cannot be attributed to the
prevalence of formal punishment by Japan's organizations in their dealings with courageous managers. The
overall pattern of organizational response to a courageous
act, regardless of its success or failure, is remarkably the
same as in the United States.: 51% of the time nothing
happened, 23% of the time courageous Japanese managers received a positive organizational response, and
23% of the time they received a negative one. Thus,
there is no evidence that Japanese organizations were unusual in stifling courage through punishment. In fact,
when we look at Japanese organizational responses to an
act's success or failure we find evidence to the contrary.
Here, for the first time, the pattern departs sharply from
that of American companies. There were two differences.

First, failure in Japan is likely to be less costly to a
courageous manager, by a lot. Look at the figures:

Organizational response to failure	In the United States	In Japan
Nothing	44%	75%
Positive	0	0
Negative	56%	25%

Once again, the evidence points away from overt, brutish
hierarchical constraint. In comparison to their American

counterparts, Japanese organizations were about half as likely to punish managers whose courageous initiatives failed. In Japan, such overtly punishing organizational measures are socially unacceptable and, I believe, largely unnecessary because the forces of continuity are aided by the more subtle constraints of peer group influence and culturally induced individual dispositions. In the end, Japanese managers constrain themselves from acts of courage and are self-punishing when such "misadventures" occur.

The second difference between Japanese and American firms' responses to success and failure serves as an illustration of the constraint and the self-punishment: 22% of the Japanese managers whose courageous acts **succeeded** report that they "felt obliged" to resign from their organizations. They were not fired. Nevertheless, they all report their feeling that they had to leave. One said his behavior was "embarrassing." It caused "disruption," said another. Such feelings and behavior find no parallel among American managers. Not one American manager resigned, for any reason, when his or her courageous act succeeded. I believe that these dramatic differences between Japanese and American managers reflect the existence, within the Japanese, of powerful internal forces acting to stifle nonnormative, individual behavior.

Evidence of these forces is also contained in the responses of Japanese managers to a question about why their attempts to influence others succeeded. Nearly all of those who believed that they had succeeded in influencing others attributed their success to being **trusted** and **popular.** American managers were in considerably less agreement about why their influence attempts succeeded. Interestingly, the most frequently given reason (it was offered by only about half the group), was that "I had the support of **powerful** people." Thus, in Japan, social relationships were seen as the reason that influence attempts succeeded, while in the United States the backing of authority was seen as primary.

Nippon: The Land and Its People provides a simple and direct summary of these findings when it says,

> Conformity is the norm in Japanese society. . . . In contrast to Western people who are more likely to express their opinions openly in a self-asserting way, Japanese tend to speak and act only after due consideration has been given to the other person's feelings and point of view.

Kenichi Takemura is called a **hyoron-ka,** or critic-at-large, in Japan. Golden quotes him as saying of his land and its people,

> In most countries, particularly in the West, each person has his own individualistic ideas, so he doesn't have to be taught. . . . But Japanese, who have been trained by social obligation and custom not to be individualistic, have lost their ability to think for themselves.

Takemura's unqualified claims about "the Japanese" as well as my own are, of course, exaggerations. Nevertheless, they serve to accurately illustrate the cause and consequence of different **tendencies** in Japanese and American organizational life.

The array of data and the comments of the Japanese, and of American observers of the Japanese scene, lead me to conclude that the relatively infrequent reporting of courage by Japanese managers is not simply the result of Japanese humility and a consequent unwillingness to boast about courageous behavior. I believe that Japanese organizations provide physical opportunities for the occurrence of managerial courage, but employ managerial tactics which amplify culturally induced tendencies to conform. In a supreme effort to create involvement, manage what they imagine to be disharmonizing friction, and capitalize on the cultural disposition to give dedicated service, the Japanese system of organizational problem solving and decision making has become an extraordinary means of organization maintenance, but not of organization regeneration. It provides continuous opportunity to do better, but not an encouraging means of doing differently. In Japanese organizational life, continuity and conformity dominate over discontinuity and courage.

In the cultural matrix of Japan this domination has been anything but a disaster. Why? For an answer I will tell a short story about **Matsushita,** Japan's industrial giant. It illustrates how Japanese organizations have used these dominant cultural tendencies to great advantage. **Matsushita** began with an electrical plug that the company's founder, Konosuke Matsushita, adapted and marketed, undercutting rivals' prices by 30%. The plug was not a better mousetrap; it possessed no preciously practical innovation; it was just cheaper. The tradition inaugurated with that plug has continued: Once a market exists, **Matsushita** arrives with a slightly different, less expensive edition of products that others have developed. The tradition has turned the company into a giant, reputed to have 14,000 products, produced in 39 manufacturing operations, and sold through 28 sales companies in 130 countries. Strange? Not at all. Read what Lohr, in his article about Matsushita, had to say about this business strategy, which some have labeled the "followership" approach:

> Japanese companies as a whole have employed the strategy, in one form or another, in industry after industry. Often latecomers, they have used astute marketing techniques, product differentiation and lowcost manufacturing as the keys to international success in such businesses as motorcycles, television and cars.

Matsushita, a classic example of Japanese management practice, is compared to Harold Geneen's autocratically controlled IT&T by Richard Pascale and Anthony Athos in their book, *The Art of Japanese Management.* They say:

> Interestingly, neither Matsushita nor IT&T has excelled in major breakthroughs in basic or applied research. There are no tales in these tightly controlled firms of inventive heroes who courageously stuck to

one product like Xerography or Polaroid cameras until faith was rewarded.

Although there were different styles of tight control at these two firms, both apparently discouraged acts of courage. **Matsushita's** style gently fostered an adaptive, conforming managerial posture. Playing on peer group pressure and culturally induced individual disposition, it encouraged people to do better, but not to do differently. IT&T's managers, it would seem, were motivated by fear of reprisal for failure from a punishing hierarchy. They avoided risky, unconventional alternatives, took the safe paths and sometimes lost opportunity for creative innovation. Thus, for different reasons, the costs of courage and the pressures to conform were high in both these settings.

The Japanese are not complacent about conformity in their organizations. Most (89%) of those with whom I "spoke" said **more courage** would be better. Sono Fukujiro, president of TDK Electronics, helps me to explain these statistics when he says, "Japan's history up to now has been one of imitation; there's been no real technology or creativity." He continues by warning that "although Japan has succeeded up to now by applying technology and inventions borrowed from abroad, from now on it will have to bring its originality into full play." Lohr, in his June 1982 *New York Times* article, arrives at the same conclusion: "Perhaps most important, the country's emphasis on conformity, obedience and uniformity, all of which have been crucial to its highly efficient assembly lines, has discouraged individual creativity and, with it, far-reaching product inventions." He continues by expressing concern about Japan's ability to invent:

> Success in this area will be among the most important factors for the nation's economic future and, many say, the acid test of its society. Japan has come up with precious few basic contributions to scientific theory or breakthrough technologies. To date, its innovative skill has been in refining, repackaging or miniaturizing existing technologies.

The paradoxical conjecture here is that the very same organizational culture and management technique that helped when organization growth required order and conformity will hurt when further progress requires diversity and creative individual initiative.

My data offer a mixed message about the Japanese response to this potential need for more diversity and creative individual initiative. Looking at trends in the frequency of courageous acts over the past two decades, there is nothing to indicate that courage is on the upswing in Japan. In fact, the trend line is flat, with no increases or decreases. But when we look at the fate of courageous acts in Japan, that is, their success or failure, the pattern that emerges provokes speculation.

Before 1974, about three-fourths of the courageous acts by Japanese managers succeeded. In the turbulent 1975 to 1977 period, immediately after the oil crisis, 100% of courageous acts failed. After 1978, however, the pattern completely reverses and almost every manager who acted courageously during this most recent period reports success. So, in that watershed period after 1974, Japanese organizations, like American ones, may have hunkered down, but only for an instant. They rose quickly, and have been increasingly open and responsive to managerial acts of courage ever since. Thus, once again, we see evidence that Japanese organizations—in actual, statistical terms—are actively accepting courageous behavior, but the occurrence of such behavior is dependent on the initiative of individual Japanese managers, and they are apparently being stifled by culturally induced social pressures and their own individual dispositions.

It may be that, in time, the increased rate of success for courageous acts will stimulate more individual acts of courage in Japan. The possibility is supported by some spotty evidence that Japan is changing in directions that are similar to Western countries, with individuals showing greater nonconformity: Arrests for drug abuse increased more than 20 times between 1970 and 1980; juvenile crime rose 48% between 1978 and 1979, while all other crime rates declined; more than 50% of Japanese women over 15 years of age are now working and 57% of working women are married; and, there is an urban population whose kids increasingly go to day-care centers, watch color television and want luxuries.

Evidence of Japan's apparent change confronted me in March 1983, during my most recent visit to that nation. At the time, newspapers were filled with stories about students physically abusing teachers. Hardly what one was accustomed to expect in that orderly, respectful society. Also, during that same visit, I spent many hours discussing an affirmative action problem that Japanese organizations are having with the descendents of a group whose members in feudal times were called "nonhumans." Another dramatic illustration of the changes that may be occurring in Japan was revealed in a survey taken in 1980, which reversed the finding of a 1960 survey showing that, in 1980, 71% of Japanese between the ages of 15 and 19 said that they wanted an individual lifestyle, while fewer than 10% said that they were motivated to lead lives which are useful to society. Further, today's Japanese workers are less likely than in the past to forego vacation, or to work overtime or during weekends. In 1980, for example, this lessening of group loyalty was illustrated when 80 computer technicians left jobs at Ishikawajima-Harima Heavy Industry—they build ships and machinery—to open their own consulting firm. That's big news in Japan.

Robert Christopher, who wrote an article on the "Changing Face of Japan," says that things there are "worse," yes, but they are not at all bad by comparison to Western nations. The changing standards and increasing nonconformity should not be mistaken as indications of Japan's decline. Christopher prognosticates: "What will emerge from this process, it seems safe to predict, is a 'softer' more individualistic Japan—which will still boast the most purposeful and productive society of any great industrial nation in the world."

He may be right. Japan may be well on its way toward

changing the society in a direction that further blends East and West, by stimulating more diversity and creative individual initiative. That may seem like an impossible transformation, but such turnabouts are not unknown in the history of Japanese society. In 1853, for example, Japan's somewhat shaky feudal state ended almost two centuries of isolation. The event is associated with the arrival of Commodore Perry and the U.S. Navy. A new government was formed under the Emperor Meiji 15 years later, and within 20 years the recently feudal state was a formidable, Westernized contender in the Industrial Revolution. On that occasion the community's tight hold over individual behavior permitted a comparatively rapid and radical transformation. Now, approximately 100 years later, the problem that Japan may be facing is paradoxical: The question is, can this **natto** society use its tendencies towards conformity to transform itself into a place of greater diversity and individual initiative?

What is the implication of Japan's success for industry elsewhere in the world? Some say "forget it." They claim that evidence for the successful applicability of Japanese management techniques is impressionistic and without the benefit of any scientifically controlled research. They point out that we cannot know for sure that Japan's commercial success has been a consequence of Japanese management style. Too much else was occurring: Japan benefited from a vast postwar reconstruction which allowed it to modernize its industrial base, with the result that the average age of U.S. plants and equipment is approximately 10 years older than Japan's; Japanese enterprise benefits from an unusually close collaboration with government; Japanese companies enjoy unique relationships with their unions; Japanese firms are very likely to be family owned; Japanese employees retire at an early age; and, Japanese methods of funding businesses are typically different from those used in the United States.

These facts cannot be denied, nor can their causal role in the Japanese success story be firmly established. The fact is that no one can safely pinpoint the exact weight that should be assigned to the different causes of Japan's business ascendancy during the past few decades. It is brazen to claim that Japanese management techniques are **the** cause of Japan's success, and it is impudent to claim that they are not **a** cause. The rest of the world should not forget what the Japanese have done, for there is value in the example, but it cannot afford to blindly attempt mimicry of that experience. The Japanese approach to management both reflects and benefits from the cultural context of Japan. It supports and feeds on existing culturally induced dispositions. That, paradoxically, is its strength and its weakness.

Chapter Seven

Guidelines for Individual Success and Survival

"The Trick Is Knowing What To Do and How and When To Do It"

Oh stay with company and mirth
And daylight and the air;
Too full already is the grave
Of fellows that were good and brave
And died because they were.

These lines are from the poem "A Shropshire Lad," which was written by Alfred Edward Houseman. His somber message easily applies to organization life where metaphorical corporate graveyards are also "too full" with the "remains" of managers who were brave, **and died because they were.** Their tombs, such as they are, lend power to the poem's advice to "stay with company and mirth," avoiding open commitment to any controversial issue. The powerful sway of that advice on individual managers, however, may be disproportionate to the actual costs which accrue as a consequence of courageous behavior. The reality is that nearly two-thirds of the courageous acts reported to me succeeded, and only 20% of the managers who acted courageously reported suffering any negative outcome as a consequence of their efforts. Managerial courage is not synonymous with career suicide.

Of course, if you happen to be among the one-in-three whose ideas are disregarded, or among the one-in-five who suffer some negative outcome, it is certainly no fun. Working toward minimizing the likelihood of falling into these unfortunate groups is properly an aim of any manager who acts courageously. Courage is no less noble or organizationally beneficial if the actor survives. On the

contrary, the example of a courageous manager who suc-
ceeds, even thrives, much more than the example of one
who fails and is punished, is likely to stimulate others to
behave courageously, thereby increasing the possibility
of benefit to the organization. The trick is being successful and surviving is knowing **what** to do as well as **how** and
when to do it.

The courageous managers in my group who lived on
to enjoy "company and mirth, and daylight and the air"
acted in accord with some, or all, of the following five
guidelines:

1. Watch your focus
2. Watch your credibility
3. Be direct
4. Create supporters, not saboteurs, by regulating
    tone, tempo, and threat
5. Propose solutions to problems that have caused
    pain

Watch Your Focus

The battleground on which a courageous act occurs affects the likelihood of its success. A purist might say,
"That should not be so. On each occasion a courageous
act should stand or fall only on the merits of the case, regardless of the focus of concern." Perhaps that should be
the case, but it seems not to be. Change the focus of con-

cern and you change not only the risk of ideacide but also the likelihood of a positive or negative organizational response to success or failure. If we look at the statistics, we can easily see how the downside risk of failure and the upside potential of a positive organizational response both changed as the focus of a courageous managerial act shifted from **subordinate behavior** to **business issues, ethical matters,** and **the performance of superiors.**

A focus on **subordinates** presented the safest downside risk, but there was no upside potential. Everyone who focused on subordinates succeeded at being heard, but organizations didn't seem to care—nothing happened, neither positive (e.g., a promotion or some other perk) nor negative (e.g., a demotion, firing, or forced resignation).

A focus on **business** issues involved some small downside risk (27% of these managers experienced ideacide), but there was enormous upside potential: 93% of the positive organization responses to courageous acts occurred when the focus was on business issues and 49% of managers who focused on business issues received a positive organization response.

A focus on **ethical** matters produced a downside risk (42% of the efforts met with ideacide) without any compensating upside potential: Not one of the managers who focused on ethical matters received a positive organizational response.

A focus on **the performance of superiors** had the greatest downside risk (53% suffered ideacide) and there was only a very small upside potential: 7% received a positive organizational response, while almost 30% suffered a negative one, more than occurred in the case of any other focus.

The message to managers who want to maximize potential benefits and minimize potential costs is clear: You are safest sticking to business issues, or framing your concern as a business issue. No other focus comes close to providing the same chance of a positive organization response.

Watch Your Credibility

Managers from different functions are not equally successful in dealing with different issues. Overall, people employed in **line and operation** functions tend to be most successful. Regardless of the focus of their effort, about 75% of them report that their courageous initiatives were appropriately explored and experimented with. By comparison, the least successful people were from **sales and marketing** functions, where only a bit more than 60% reported success. **Staff** people and those in **general management** fell in between, reporting success rates of 67 and 68%, respectively. Breaking down these overall patterns still further suggests the intriguing possibility that

functional groups have different strengths and weak-
nesses:

Line and operations people, for example, were the
only ones who succeeded in having their case heard
when the focus was on ethical matters. In fact their rec-
ord was a perfect 100%.

Sales and marketing managers, in this sample, divided
their focus between business issues and the performance of superiors. They succeeded 80% of the time
with business issues and **never** when they focused on
superiors' performance.

Staff people did better than any other group when the
focus was on the performance of superiors. They reported success a spectacular 89% of the time compared
to a 53% average for the total group.

General management personnel reported 100% success when the focus was on business issues. The next
most successful groups were line and operations, and
sales and marketing, who report success rates of 86 and
80%, respectively. Staff people did least well when
business issues were the focus, reporting a success rate
of only 63%, which is a worse performance than they
had when their focus was on that most treacherous of
topics, the performance of superiors.

Evidently the connection between focus and functional role cannot be safely overlooked by managers

who act courageously. The alignment of the two certainly seems to be affecting the likelihood of one's success and survival. As a guide, managers might ask themselves, "Is the focus of this effort one which causes my image in the organization to enhance the credibility of my case or hinder it?" Generally speaking, credibility is affected by image in two ways. The first, obviously, is acknowledged expertise. Notice, for example, how staff people fall down, just a bit, on business issues, an area in which everyone else does so well; but also notice how they do so well when the issue concerns performance of superiors, a domain where everyone should fear to tread. The second way in which image affects credibility has to do with predictability. If a focus is uncommon for a person, and untainted by signs of self-interest, then onlookers are less likely to say, "Oh, there he or she goes again," and are more likely to credit the effort with credibility, believing that, "He or she wouldn't be acting that way if it weren't especially important."

Maintaining credibility is central to the success and survival of courageous managers. Therefore, when managers decide to challenge what is, prudence requires attention to the alignment of their image in the organization and the focus of their concern. When their alignment is right, credibility increases and the likelihood of success is enhanced; when their alignment is wrong, credibility decreases and success may be more at the mercy of **how** you give voice to your dissent and **when** you do it.

Be Direct

Courageous managers stated their visions of what might be in two different ways, **directly** or **indirectly**. Those who acted **directly** either took immediate action and did what they believed was right, despite opposition or, lacking the ability, power or opportunity to do that, they stood face-to-face with opposing parties, openly proclaiming their different ideas. In contrast, the efforts of courageous managers who acted **indirectly** were drawn out and protracted. Letters, reports, and memorandums formed the core of their strategy. Their relationship with the opposition was more at arm's length, and their efforts never involved any self-initiated implementation of the proposed action.

Of the courageous efforts that managers reported to me 43% were **direct** and 57% were **indirect**. Different fates awaited these two groups and in the difference lies an important message for all managers.

If you are going to act courageously, then act with determination and decisiveness. Do not equivocate. Be certain and definite. Act with conviction. Organizations yield more readily to direct action. Only 20% of the courageous managers who acted directly failed, but more than twice that proportion, 48%, failed when they took indirect action.

Once success occurred, direct action continued to provide benefits to courageous managers. Those who took direct action and succeeded enjoyed a positive organizational response 71% of the time. If they took indirect action, however, then, despite success, their organizations accorded them a positive response only 20% of the time. Failure does not greatly change the relative benefit of direct over indirect action. When courageous efforts failed, managers were neither better nor worse off because they acted directly. In the final analysis, if a courageous effort is direct then (1) the likelihood of success is greater, (2) in all probability success will be followed by some tangible, positive organizational response, and (3) should failure occur, you will be no worse off than if you had acted indirectly. Be direct!

Caution. In Japan this advice does not apply and may be hazardous to your health. Approximately 8 out of 10 Japanese managers acted indirectly. What is more to the point, if a Japanese manager acted **directly,** failure was just as likely as success. If he acted **indirectly,** however, success was more than twice as likely as failure. The results are very nearly a mirror image of what happened in the United States. The two nations seem to be on opposite sides of the world in more ways than one.

The benefits of direct, courageous action in the United States cannot be set aside by claiming that managers who took direct action focused on safer issues than those who acted indirectly. They did not. There were no discernable differences in focus between the two groups. Why then is direct action so advantageous? The research of two French scholars (Claude Faucheux and Serge Moscovici) provides an answer that has important practical value for managerial survival. They investigated the occasions on which minority opinions influenced the views of larger majorities. Their findings lead to the conclusion that obvious and consistent perseverance enhances minority influence, probably because it communicates the minority's confidence, certainty, and commitment. When people who are not written off as weird take direct action, they are more likely to be taken seriously. The salience and intensity of their act encourages others to see them as dedicated, embracing a sense of mission. Through this, their vision of what might be becomes more compelling because onlookers endow it with greater **credibility** (an old friend). "They wouldn't behave that way," one says, "unless there was something to what they believe."

Create Supporters, Not Saboteurs, by Regulating Tone, Tempo, and Threat

Peter Drucker has said, "Whenever anything is being accomplished it is being done, I have learned, by a monomaniac with a mission." I disagree. Personal commitment to a mission has persuasive effects on a group but, I have learned, there is no need for monomania. In fact, the managers that I met who took direct action seemed to be anything but impulsive, raving, or fanatic. There was in their behavior persistence, but not blind obstinacy. They persevered, but they were not egotistically recalcitrant.

In my view the tactics of successful courageous man-

agers were revealed in a study published in 1982 by Warner Schilit and Edwin Locke, in the *Administrative
Science Quarterly*. It was titled, "A Study of Upward Influence in Organizations." Two of the most important tac-
tical factors affecting the success of upward influence in
organizations were identified as the persistence of the actor and the development of a logical presentation in his
or her arguments. The following quote from one successful manager who acted directly illustrates the point:

> My boss never had responsibility. He wasn't really
> able to manage me and the business that I was run-
> ning, which was an unusual one for the company. I was
> concerned about the specific directions I was being
> told to take in running the business. In several dis-
> cussions I told him of my concerns, carefully putting
> out the problem, details, numbers, the works. Some-
> times he listened. More often than not he didn't. He
> told me, "No, this is the way you'll do this."
>
> This fellow had no idea of things that would go into
> Management 101. He was bright enough, but just
> didn't have the experience, and he made it worse by
> not listening to me or others. Finally, on one trans-
> action, I said "No, I won't do it." I was going to leave,
> but then decided to do something about it. I thought
> about it for a long time, then I went to the president
> and laid it out. The whole issue, numbers, etc., you
> know, all the data. He listened but gave very little
> feedback. I hung in. He had to understand. Finally he
> said, "Thank you. I appreciate it."

A second manager's story also shows how successful, direct, courageous efforts incorporate these important tactics of upward influence.

I was working against senior executives in order to defend ideas that were concerned with how to deal with the company's human resources. We were building a new facility in a rural area and needed, let's say, 300 people. They had to be recruited, selected, hired, and trained. We had thousands of applicants. The problem was to sift through them. But what criteria, procedure should be used? The regular procedure was to have line people sift through applications and select. There was nepotism, prejudice, and lots of incompetence. It was not satisfactory. I said "no." Senior executives clearly wanted to go back to the established procedure. The line managers wanted to and the personnel department wanted to. Hell, except for the president who agreed with me, but wouldn't say a word, I was out there by myself. It was cold.

It went on for a while. I met with everyone saying what I thought. They said what they thought. While we were talking I set up a procedure. It wasn't ideal, but it was a massive change. It was objective—more so, anyway. It stressed the company's need to get competent people. I went ahead; there was no real agreement, but I had to do the right thing without losing them . . . you get a little piece at a time. Try to get it all and you get nothing. . . . There was a lot of risk. The VP's and the line managers could get me. The president could not have saved me. If enough people will not work with you, you're finished.

This quote also illustrates how the acceptance of courageous initiatives depends on having enough people believe that the outcome will give them a place in the organization after a change occurs. When ideas for change are presented in a way that threatens the sense of security experienced by important constituencies as rapidly as it reduces the upset that they are feeling from the prospect of unresolved problems, the chances of the ideas being adopted are severely reduced.

Successfully courageous managers who took direct action signaled their strong sense of mission, but tempered their devotion by remaining appropriately responsive to the condition of constituencies and the practical need to have supporters, not saboteurs. These managers tended to be zealous, but not brash or abrasive. There was no swaggering, "shoot it out quality" to them. Their persistence had a quiet orderliness to it. They addressed themselves to issues, not people. Unpossessed by any raging fanaticism, they were free to acknowledge the legitimacy of opposing positions without diluting the integrity of their own dreams of what might be. By showing concern for an organization's continued welfare, while persistently offering alternatives to existing policy, procedure, or commitment in ways that were sympathetic to the threats that might be experienced by others, successfully courageous managers cultivated alliances. Finally, their courageous efforts were not explosively out-of-control. They exhibited a sense of timing and a concern with **when** to act courageously.

Propose Solutions to Problems That Have Caused Pain

The comments of successfully courageous managers frequently display strategic considerations about timing that seem hardly evident in the remarks made by other managers who were equally courageous, but demonstrably unsuccessful. For example, Charles T., an engineer with an MBA, told me about the time that he spoke out in favor of discontinuing a few of his company's traditional products and divesting the related manufacturing sites. These facilities, he said, always seemed like "religious shrines, with landmark status."

> Why did I do it? Well, hell, the time was right. It wasn't a new thing with me. I could see it coming for 18 months, maybe two years. But it was a question of opportunity. Conditions were changing—visibly—the market was changing. The labor pool was changing. It was confusing, upsetting, the right time to push the point. What they were doing wasn't working and not one of them had a new idea.

Charles T.'s colleagues and superiors were experiencing significant discomfort. He recognized that and played on it.

When I spoke up—I'll never forget it was a. . . . This miserable, raining June day—everyone sat tight-lipped, sort of grim. My God, the rain sounded like a herd of horses. Man, was I scared; you know, I was young. Most of these people had put their blood into the things that I was just about tearing down. I tried to say how it was all important; how the company image and history was involved—it was true, but we had to do something about the problem. It was sure to kill us sooner or later. That was the thing. I tried to speak out about the losses. They were really there. No one could say different. I didn't want the old guard to start storming, and figured I would stay with that—the losses.

Ultimately, Charles T.'s efforts succeeded. His sense of timing was right. People were uneasy about the company's traditional methods, despite their adherence to it. Charles sensed the developing ambivalence and used it to guide his effort. The action implication is clear: Courageous managers who propose solutions to problems that as yet have caused little pain cannot be optimistic about their chances of success.

Waiting for the discomfort to mount may provide a second benefit. It increases the opportunity for the splintering of majority opinion, a propitious omen for acts of managerial courage. One manager said to me,

By the time I arrived they were at each other. Nothing was working and the blame was being passed around like a hot potato. They were frustrated and it weakened their opposition. They weren't united. That made it easier.

As this example illustrates, by avoiding a premature engagement of the issue, successfully courageous managers sometimes allow the "yea-sayers" to try all the standard, traditional solutions. Their failure weakens the forces of continuity and the status quo, thereby enhancing the strength of courageous endeavors which offer nontraditional solutions to exceptional, even unprecedented problems. Often, the exceptional or unprecedented character of an organization's problem is disguised in familiar-looking garb, and its novelty becomes apparent only after traditional efforts at solution prove futile. Patiently waiting for that to happen may be a cherished virtue for courageous managers to possess. Monomaniacal impatience and impulsiveness simply will not do.

I am not naive. Waiting for the discomfort to build, the majority to splinter, or the yea-sayers to futilely run through their bag of conventional tricks is not always an easy option. While waiting for the right moment to act, costs are being incurred which may be harmful, perhaps fatally harmful, to organization survival. Every courageous manager must mentally balance these risks against the increased risk of failure which is incurred if the timing is wrong. There is no gain if a courageous act fails and the manager does not survive the attempt.

In that classic tale of bravery and foolishness, *Don Quixote,* Miguel de Cervantes wrote, "The brave man carves out his fortune." By maintaining the right focus, approach, and timing courageous managers may indeed be able to carve out their fortunes. But the carving will be imperfect; while attempts to enhance the probability of success are possible, it is impossible to guarantee that happy outcome. However attentive they are to the guidelines offered here, managers must not fail to recognize that their fates are going to be profoundly affected by the character and culture of their organizations. For, if it is true that brave people carve out their own fortunes, then it is equally true that organizations frequently carve up brave people, much to the organization's eventual misfortune.

Chapter Eight

Guidelines for Corporate Survival

"The Crux of American Corporate Inventiveness Is Risk Taking."

A s I sit at my desk writing this book's final chapter, I am very aware of an event that occurred almost five years ago in an office hundreds of feet above Manhattan's midtown streets. The room's aroma, its sweet-burnt odor of pipe tobacco, the papers, books, and other clutter, my soft chair and feeling of ease, all seem remarkably close despite the passing of many more than a thousand days. I was sitting in the office of one of my client company's most senior executives. His slightly rumpled appearance and avuncular manner were familiar to the point of being comforting. It is easy for me to hurdle the time that has passed in order to recreate in my mind his thoughtful, confident answer to the first question of the needs analysis survey that we were conducting:

> Beginning right now, organization success and survival will depend on challenging what we've been doing, on confronting existing organizational strategies, practices and policy. It will require us to make certain that . . . key managers act courageously, telling us what's wrong, and not cower in organizational corners, vainly hoping that necessary changes will magically occur without their involvement.

He was speaking of his organization and its "fast-trackers," but his message applies to us all, perhaps more so now than before.

Do not misunderstand. No one is advocating that there is a panacea for all of business' ills. Managerial courage alone will guarantee neither organizational excellence nor national economic success, but its role in achieving those goals can be paramount. Acts of managerial courage have the capability of alerting firms to both their options and failings. Like a ship's gyroscope, courageous acts provide course corrections by sending signals to receptive organizations. Such corrections are essential because competitive advantage in business is almost always temporary. The complex matrix of production, marketing, finance, and personnel that led to success yesterday and today ages quickly, often becoming a poor fit for tomorrow's work. Alfred E. Sloan identified this unrelenting cycle of organizational obsolescence in his book, *My Years with General Motors,* when he wrote:

> The circumstances of ever-changing market and ever-changing product are capable of breaking any business organization if that organization is unprepared for change—indeed, in my opinion, if it has not provided procedures for anticipating change.

Preservation of a competitive advantage in business requires firms to do things differently, innovating beyond yesterday's and today's successes. Doing things differently requires imagination and the pursuit of uncommon, even unprecedented, innovations. It requires human resources to be managed in ways that stimulate, rather than stifle managerial courage, otherwise stagnation will occur and the competition more likely lost. Effective management of human resources requires more than shuffling hanging boxes on an organization chart, changing titles, lines of authority, and job descriptions. For courageous, innovative initiatives to occur, those men and women who are charged with the responsibility of corporate survival must learn to recognize and then manage the inevitable tension between the forces of continuity and discontinuity.

At Intel, one of the United States' more visible companies, the problem that I have been discussing was recognized by its 44-year-old president when he was quoted by Lohr as saying:

> I can't pretend to know the shape of the next generation of silicon or computer technology anymore. That's why people like me need the knowledge from the people closest to the technology. That's why we can't have hierarchical barriers to an exchange of ideas and information that you have at so many corporations.

In managing the balance between the forces of continuity and discontinuity, however, constricting hierarchy is only one-half the problem. The other half, the part overlooked in the statement, is that, under the right circumstances, groups, acting through a tyranny of the majority, are able to stifle ideas and information just as easily and as finally as an oppressive, autocratic boss. Indeed, the danger posed by groups may be even more pernicious. First, because it is an unavoidable consequence of bringing human beings together in order to do some work, and second, it is less resisted because it often operates through a subtle, smothering embrace, rather than obvious and hateful oppression.

Production systems always create powerful social/psychological commitments which must be breeched if change is to occur. Alliances to preserve the status quo are not simply rooted in the conservative momentum generated by invested funds, or in the self-protective desire not to abandon what was once endorsed, lest it be interpreted as an admission of error and defeat. These alliances are also founded on profound, often unrecognized social/psychological processes that inevitably result from living and working together with others. People come to like what is familiar and, if they feel positively about their fellows, they come to accept their beliefs about what is right and wrong, good and bad. A leveling occurs as people bend to fit the mold and avoid disharmony. Even groups which were initially innovative, perhaps radical, mature with time. Their once innovative ideas become rigid dogma and their previously courageous deviants, conservative reactionaries. Ultimately, change is resisted, and constancy—the old way—is pursued, sometimes in directions that are counterproductive to future organization success.

The obstacles to be overcome in an organizational search for remedy are formidable, but not insurmountable. Regeneration in organizations is not biologically determined. It is essentially a malleable social process. Even decisions involving technical and financial change have unavoidably social components, with human beings trying to interpret inconclusive "facts" while they are simultaneously being swayed this way and that by the need to preserve and protect their prestige, power, and turf. Despite its essentially social nature, however, in metaphorical terms, organization regeneration does appear to possess the overtones of an evolutionary process. From this perspective, managerial courage advances organizational evolution by stimulating innovative organizational experiments. Some of these experiments produce successfully adaptive, regenerative change, providing organizations with the competitive edge that they need. Organizations which stifle courage and prevent experimenting, therefore, are unprepared for change and decrease their chances of having that edge. Sealed in the cement of rigid habit, they increase the probability of their own extinction. Without plasticity and flexibility (or extra-organizational intervention by the likes of government), chances are that they will eventually lose out to heartier, more adaptable competitors just as soon as the environment changes in ways that are unsuited to their specialized, unchanging way of being.

Organizational survival and growth depend on having and using a variety of ideas. Ideacide—the murder of an idea prematurely, before it is appropriately and adequately tested—is not only a bruise to individual dignity, it is a potential threat to organizational survival. Ideacide stifles courage. It discourages courageous initiative by preordaining its futility and deters it by raising the potential costs to unacceptable levels. Practical considerations and the conservative-tending psychology of groups together cause a natural organizational drift toward idea-cide that is impossible to fully prevent. Courage, therefore, is always necessary. There is never a time when dissent from the current consensus is risk-free. Organizations need to work at limiting ideacide in order to provide a more hospitable environment for managerial doings. It is a pragmatically essential condition for the future of every organization.

By themselves, organizational mottos and slogans do little to discourage ideacide or promote managerial courage. Admonitions like:

Managers must keep an open mind

Managers must reward innovations, so that innovation rewards them

Managers bound by tradition, traditionally are bound to fail

have little value in the absence of tangible organizational support.

There is a simple principle involving the separation of organizational responsibilities which guides successful organizational efforts to limit ideacide: "**Separate the responsibility of maintaining daily operations, the status quo, from the responsibility of generating ideas different from those of the status quo.**"

If ideas which dissent from the established practice are compelled to flow through channels that were structured and staffed to implement and reward behavior consistent with established practice, then the likelihood that the ideas will receive safe passage is severely curtailed. New, parallel channels are needed. The staffing of these channels must be with personnel whose vested interests are in securing productive, new ideas. The channels need to be structured to provide for a safe, efficient flow of new ideas to decision makers, one that develops promising possibilities, and turns back less promising ones, after affording them a hearing and without punishing their authors. Three organizationally successful ways of creating these new channels have been through the use of **sponsor, structures,** and **reward systems.** These three groups of organizational tools for supporting courage are not independent conceptually, nor mutually exclusive, in practice. They are simply a convenient way of talking about some general approaches that have had practical value.

Sponsors

Organizational **godfathers** represent one means of achieving a separation between organizational responsibilities for today's operations and tomorrow's developments. Godfathers have the explicit responsibility for receiving, assessing, and shepherding ideas through the system, hence their designation as "sponsors." Because their prestige and success are both linked to the production of ideas, sponsors are less likely to commit ideacide or respond defensively to acts of managerial courage. In important ways access to sponsors who have some discretionary power and reduced investment in how things currently are, recreates the culture of a small growing company which is hungry for innovation and comparatively unconstrained by committed investments, and where employees have a more direct line to senior people without wading through entangling red tape.

Texas Instruments **TI** reports using a form of this approach in a program called IDEA. In a 1982 article in *Business Horizons,* Shelby McIntyre says that **TI**s sponsors, who are called "individual contributors," have the power to finance the development of new business ideas, up to a specified limit, without executive approval. This arrangement has the potential of providing an avenue and an impetus for proposing long-shot projects. A related idea comes from a 1980 article by Robert Brown in *Management Review,* "When a Business Matures: How To Keep the Entrepreneurial Thrust." Brown was a vice president at Seatrains when he wrote the piece suggesting that organizations have an **entrepreneurial ombudsman.** An ombudsman would provide others with a means of by-passing conventional, formal organizational structures and procedures. He or she would receive ideas, perhaps advise and guide their development, and then take them directly to senior management, using the ombudsman's privileged route.

The role that an **entrepreneurial ombudsman** might play is not terribly dissimilar to the role occasionally played by consultants. They, too, receive ideas and pass them along, moving outside and around the formal organization. When they are seen as unbiased and as possessing relevant expertise, the ideas that consultants pass along gain in credibility, gaining a hearing that they might otherwise not receive. Having this role permanently built into an organization—by using the **entrepreneurial ombudsman** idea, for example—is an intriguing possibility. If the position existed and an organization so desired, the ombudsman's job could easily be expanded beyond that of being a conduit only for new product ideas to include passing along remedial ideas and concerns about any organizationally dysfunctional policy, procedure, or performance.

The strength of the ombudsman approach is that it provides a safe channel for trafficking ideas to senior management. Its shortcoming is that, unlike TIs individual contributors program, it leaves final approvals to those who occasionally may be under great pressure to avoid risks and protect the status quo. Of course, an approach like TI's also has its vulnerability. In order to be successful, sponsors need to have the reputation of someone who is accessible, unbiased, and credible, as well as a personal orientation which allows them to respond more to a proposal's merits than its acceptability to powerful others. A sponsor's success is also enhanced when an organization provides him or her with (1) **protection** from those who inevitably will be affected by ideas that are advanced and (2) **rewards** when the ideas advanced prove organizationally beneficial.

Structure

A second way of separating the responsibility of maintaining daily operations, the status quo, from the responsibility of producing ideas different from it, is to create distinct units whose singular purpose is the generation and, perhaps, testing of innovative proposals. The most articulate spokesperson for this approach, a man whose work I greatly admire, is Jay Gailbraith, independent organizational consultant and author. Gailbraith argues that if these special units are to be successful, they must be physically, financially, and organizationally differentiated from regular operating units. The success of think tanks and "skunk works" within companies are examples of this approach, as is the IBM Fellows program. This program provides people who are fortunate enough to be selected for it with support for five years in order to work on projects of their own choosing. During that time they are comparatively free from ordinary surveillance and from "go" or "no go" decisions using conventional criteria. In the end, if an idea proves successful, its creator may receive a special reward.

One unique variation on this theme is a "School for Intrapreneurs" operated for intracompany entrepreneurs in Sweden by the Foresight Group, who are management consultants. The school is a response to the problem of people exiting companies to start their own business ventures because their companies are unresponsive to ideas. Instead of quitting, employees in participating companies have the option of attending the

School for Intrapreneurs where they receive help in developing a business plan. Their company funds 20 days of attendance at the school. On "graduation," employees present their plans to their respective companies. In preparation for this presentation, the companies have set, in advance, criteria for acceptance of the project, for example, a positive cash flow in three years. Companies, of course, retain the option of deciding yea or nay on the proposal, just as employees remain free to choose whether to stay with the firm or go off on their own, pursuing their dreams of what might be.

Regular, organizationally sponsored, "open forums" provide still another example of creating separate organizational structures in order to embrace the flow of ideas which buck the status quo. Former Secretary of State William P. Rogers set up such a structure at the State Department in 1971. It was called the Secretary's Open Forum. The success, or perhaps the failure, of the Secretary's Open Forum (it's hard to determine which) was attested to when critics of the process used it to disseminate a paper that they titled, "The Open Forum Program: A Mockery." Difficulties with these forums, similar to the one implied by the "mockery" accusation in the title of this paper, were recognized by Rene McPherson when he was chairman of the Dana Corporation, a power equipment company. He started a forum called, "Talk Back to the Boss." McPherson was reported to have observed that, despite assurances of safety, many employees were too frightened to stand up and speak out.

I am not surprised. It's difficult to run a successful

open forum. Unlike the School for Intrapreneurs or the IBM Fellows program, talk, not action, is its **metier.** For that reason, forums may feed the fraudulent illusion that by listening something is being done. In the absence of any subsequent action, forums drain energy and contribute to stifling courageous initiative. Also, because talk is its metier, the success of forums depends a great deal on the interpersonal, rather than the business skills, of forum participants. Consequently the potential for forum discussions to degenerate into adversarial exchanges that reduce the effort's credibility are enormous. An equally difficult problem is a forum's format which demands speaking before a large audience, something that can be anxiety provoking for people even when they want to express conformity with the status quo. Forums have another problem. They lack the reward structures that are often grafted onto other approaches. More than providing a mercenary incentive for courageous action, these structures both symbolize and strengthen an organization's commitment and, therefore, they become an important determinant of the success of any effort to increase the flow of ideas.

Reward Systems

In my questionnaire I asked managers, "Would you do it again?" Would you behave courageously? Of the managers who succeeded 84% said, "Yes, I'd do it again." Managers whose courageous efforts failed were less likely to say that same thing. Only 67% of the group said that they would do the same thing again. What did discourage them even more, however, was punishment for their failure.

Managers are not stupid. They quickly learn which behaviors produce reward and which produce punishment. Of those who were treated positively, 100% said, "Yes, I'd do it again!" And, in a complete reversal, 75% of those who experienced some negative treatment by the organizations said, "No, not me. Never again!" Very clearly, through their treatment of courageous managers, organizations are regulating the likelihood that these people will ever again act courageously.

Even more dramatically, there is evidence that organizational responses to courageous initiatives affect the likelihood that others, mere onlookers, will behave courageously in the future. I asked people to tell me about the courageous acts of managers other than themselves. Then I said, "Afterwards, how was the courage of those who knew what happened affected by the event?" In all cases where **negative contagion** occurred (i.e., where other employees were described as becoming **less** courageous), managers said that the others had observed the organization punish a courageous manager whose effort failed. **Positive contagion** occurred only when success was followed by either a positive organizational response or no response whatsoever. These findings illustrate the undeniably powerful role that organizational reward systems play in regulating the occurrence of individual courageous initiative.

3M has a rule which recognizes the way in which organizational reward structures affect initiative and innovation: Each of its divisions, there are more than 40, must generate at least 25% of its income from products that were introduced during the preceding five-year period. The rule works. It has been reported that in the past few years the company has produced more than 100 new products annually, accounting for somewhere between 18 and 27% of its business.

Product champions, the innovators, come from anywhere within the company. As they begin to work on an idea, the company urges them to answer seven questions:

1. What knowledge already exists about the product idea?
2. Where does it fit into the corporation?
3. Who does the work to produce it?
4. How can its progress be evaluated?
5. Can it be profitable?
6. Does it have a technological base?
7. Is it, or can it be, patented?

Once a product shows marketplace promise, a "new venture team" is formed. It is composed of committed people from relevant departments, including an "executive champion." Executive champions are former innovators. Their job is to nurture the new venture team and protect it from intrusions that might "nip in the bud" development of the new product. Sometimes new prod-

ucts fail, even in the absence of intrusion, just because
the idea was technically or commercially unsound. If that
should happen team members may be sad, but they have
no reason to be frightened. The organization exacts no
vengeful retribution. Each team member's job security is
guaranteed. Conversely, when new products succeed,
team members succeed also. They benefit through
changes in job status and compensation which continue
to grow as the product's success grows. In addition, each
year in a public ceremony, 3M awards trophies to teams
whose products achieve special levels of commercial success.

The award is important because of what it symbolizes
and reflects: a culture in which ideacide is discouraged.
Thomas J. Peters, writing in *Hospital Forum,* attributes
an eleventh commandment to 3M, "**never kill a new
idea.**" In managing the tension between the forces of
continuity and discontinuity, this eleventh commandment clearly places the burden of proof on those who
want to kill the idea, not on those with different dreams
of what might be. It has worked for 3M. The company has
introduced more than 50,000 new products. Its success
is a prime example of how organizations must allow the
expression of foolish, even repulsive ideas, in the pragmatic hope that such tolerance will be rewarded with a
sufficient number of useful, productive ideas.

Allowing the expression of ideas is clearly not equiv-
alent to implementing every idea that comes down the
pike. Questions of implementation must be settled by the
use of technical and commercial criteria. If ideas fail to

measure up, then a reasoned rejection should occur. The psychological consequences of such a rejection, however, are distinct from those which follow suppression and punishment. People may feel disappointed after being rejected. They may even believe the decision is foolish. But they will be free from the fears of autocratic retribution, unpossessed by a stifling sense of futility, and uninfluenced by the conformists' message, "You get along by going along," all of which carry the potential of creating a dangerous, and an altogether too common, imbalance between the forces of continuity and discontinuity.

Two hundred years ago Alexis de Tocqueville looked at a new nation and worried about its future ability to manage the forces of continuity and discontinuity:

> I cannot but fear that men may arrive at such a state as to regard every new theory as a peril, every innovation as an irksome toil, every social improvement as a stepping stone to revolution, and so refuse to move altogether for fear of being moved too far. I dread . . . lest they should at last so entirely give way to a cowardly love of present enjoyment, as to lose sight of interests of future selves and those of their descendents; and prefer to glide along the easy current of life, rather than make, when it is necessary, a strong and sudden effort to higher purpose.

A more recent piece on the same topic was addressed to the stewards of corporate life. The article, titled "The New Organization Man," was written by John Thackray. He said:

The traditional and fundamental strength of American business lies in quite the opposite direction from the corporate hymn-singing and management by broad consensus of the Japanese. Rather it is individualism in tension with the organization: **that** is the crux of American corporate inventiveness, risk-taking, the will to get things done.

Some deny this view, claiming that modern organizations have grown so complex and so large that the role of individuals in producing change is extinct. They say that the idea of movers and shakers who get things done is obsolete. There is no longer room for individuals to make "a strong and sudden effort to higher purpose." I cannot agree. My data tell me that courageous individual initiative may not always be welcomed, but it is widely valued and, when it occurs, more often than not it has impact. The interviews and questionnaires that I have shared with you speak of that impact. They contain the stories of courageous managers who **have changed** the histories of their organizations. Courageous individual initiative is not obsolete. Now, as always, organization regeneration requires confronting what **is** with a dream of what might **be.** Now, as always, it requires men and women to courageously stand up and say, "Stop. The way things are in this organization is not the way they must be. Alternatives exist."

References

Chapter One

Abernathy, William J., Clark, Kim B., & Kantrow, Alan M. *Industrial Renaissance*. New York: Basic Books, 1983.

Andersen, Hans Christian. *The Emperor's New Clothes*. Boston: Houghton Mifflin, 1949.

Burns, James MacGregor. *Leadership*. New York: Harper & Row, 1978.

Commager, Henry Steele. *The American Mind*. New Haven: Yale University Press, 1950, pp. 20–21.

Cyert, Richard M. And a critique from Carnegie-Mellon, *The New York Times*, June 5, 1983, p. 2.

Drucker, Peter F. Management's new role, *Harvard Business Review*, November–December, 1969, pp. 49–54.

Golden, Arthur S. Group think in Japan, Inc., *The New York Times Magazine*, December 5, 1982, pp. 133–140.

Gorer, Geoffrey. *The American People*. New York: Norton, 1964 (revised edition).

Harshbarger, Dwight. The individual and the social order: Notes on the management of heresy and deviance in complex organizations, *Human Relations*, 1973, 26, p. 2, 251–269.

Hirschman, Albert O. *Exit, Voice and Loyalty*. Cambridge, MA: Harvard University Press, 1970.

Kennedy, John F. *Profiles In Courage*. New York: Harper & Row, 1964 (memorial edition), p. 216.

MacGregor, Roy. The nature of heroism, *Macleans*, January 12, 1981, 94, p. 28.

Moscovici, Serge, & Faucheux, Claude. Social influence, conformity bias, and the study of active minorities, in L. Berkowitz (Ed.) *Advances In Experimental Social Psychology*, Vol. 6., pp. 149–202. New York: Academic Press, 1972.

Peters, Thomas J., & Waterman, Robert H., Jr. *In Search of Excellence: Lessons from America's best run companies.* New York: Harper & Row, 1982.

Rickover, Hyman G. "Thoughts on the presidency," *The New York Times*, February 21, 1982, pp. 1–19.

Schein, Edgar H. "SMR Forum: Does Japanese management style have a message for American managers?" *Sloan Management Review*, Fall 1981, pp. 55–68.

Tocqueville, Alexis de. *Democracy in America.* New York: Mentor, 1956 (edited and abridged by Richard D. Heffner).

Whyte, William H., Jr. *The Organization Man.* New York: Simon & Schuster, 1956.

Chapter Two

Burns, James MacGregor. *Leadership.* New York: Harper & Row, 1978.

Drucker, Peter F. "Management's new role," *Harvard Business Review*, November–December 1969, pp. 49–54.

Keniston, Kenneth. *The Uncommitted: Alienated Youth In American Society.* New York: Harcourt, Brace & World, 1965.

Kirton, Michael J. "Adaptors and innovators: A description and measure," *Journal of Applied Psychology*, 1976, *61*, pp. 622–629.

Kirton, Michael J. "Adaptors and innovators in organizations," *Human Relations*, 1980, *33*, pp. 213–224.

Whyte, William H., Jr. *The Organization Man.* New York: Simon & Schuster, 1956.

Chapter Three

Abernathy, William J., Clark, Kim B., & Kantrow, Alan M. *Industrial Renaissance.* New York: Basic Books, 1983, p. 18.

References

Clutherbuck, David. "Blowing the whistle on corporate misconduct," *International Management,* 1980, *35,* pp. 1, 14–19.

Cyert, Richard M. "And a critique from Carnegie-Mellon," *The New York Times,* June 5, 1983, p. 2.

Dunbar, Roger L. M., Dutton, John M., & Torbert, William R. "Crossing mother: Ideological constraints on organizational improvements," *Journal of Management Studies,* 1982, *19,* pp. 1, 91–108.

Gerth, Jeff. "Citicorp officials defend 70's currency trading," *The New York Times,* June 28, 1983.

Harshbarger, Dwight. "The individual and the social order: Notes on the management of heresy and deviance in complex organizations," *Human Relations,* 1973, *26,* pp. 2, 251–269.

Isaacson, Walter. Reported by Bruce W. Nelan, Christopher Redman, and Evan Thomas. "The winds of reform," *Time Magazine,* March 7, 1983, pp. 12–30.

McAdams, Tony. "Speaking out in the corporate community," *Academy of Management Review,* 1977, *2,* pp. 2, 196–205.

McIntyre, Shelby, H. "Obstacles to corporate innovation," *Business Horizons,* January–February 1982, pp. 23–28.

Miceli, Marcia Parmerlee, & Near, Janet P. "The relationships among beliefs, organizational position, and whistle blowing status: A discriminant analysis," *Academy of Management Journal,* 1984, *27,* pp. 4, 687–705.

Mohr, Charles. "Arms analyst tells house panel of problems with military costs," *The New York Times,* March 4, 1983, p. 16.

Moscovici, Serge, & Faucheux, Claude. "Social influence, conformity bias, and the study of active minorities," in L. Berkowitz (Ed.) *Advances In Experimental Social Psychology,* Vol. 6., New York: Academic Press, 1972, pp. 149–202.

Rowan, Roy. "The maverick who yelled foul at Citibank," *Fortune,* January 10, 1983, pp. 46–56.

Chapter Four

Anders, George. *The Wall Street Journal,* September 25, 1984, pp. 1, 20.

Bennis, Warren. "The five key traits of successful chief executives," *International Management*, October 1981, p. 60.

Bennis, Warren. "Leadership and development," *Training and Development Journal*, October, 1981, p. 7–9.

Bennis, Warren. "Leadership: A beleaguered species?" *Organizational Dynamics*, Summer 1976, pp. 3–16.

Burns, James MacGregor. *Leadership*. New York: Harper & Row, 1978.

Burns, John F. "Soviet study urges relaxing of controls to revive economy." *The New York Times*, August 5, 1983, pp. 1, 4.

Deutsch, Morton. *The Resolution of Conflict: Constructive and destructive processes*. New Haven: Yale University Press, 1923.

Hechinger, Fred M. "Business schools criticized," *The New York Times*, April 13, 1982, pp. C1, C4.

Holusha, John. "At Ford, a quiet revolution unfolds," *The New York Times*, Business Section, September 11, 1983, p. 1, 12.

Lawrence, Paul R., & Dyer, Davis. *Renewing American Industry*. New York: Free, 1983.

Leavitt, Harold J., & Blumen-Lipman, Jean. "A case for the relational manager," *Organizational Dynamics*, Summer 1980, pp. 27–41.

Luxenberg, Stan. "Lifetime employment, U.S. style," *The New York Times*, Business Section, April 17, 1983, p. 12F.

Pascale, Richard T., & Athos, Anthony G. *The Art of Japanese Management*. New York: Warner Books, 1981.

Peters, Thomas J., & Waterman, Robert H., Jr. *In Search of Excellence: Lessons from America's best run companies*. New York: Harper & Row, 1982.

Sloan, Alfred P. *My Years with General Motors*. Garden City, NY: Doubleday, 1964.

Tocqueville, Alexis de. *Democracy in America*, Vol. 1. New York: Knopf, 1963 (the Henry Reeve text, revised by Francis Bowen and later by Phillips Bradley).

Tocqueville, Alexis de. *Democracy in America*. New York: Mentor, 1956 (edited and abridged by Richard D. Heffner).

Whyte, William H., Jr. *The Organization Man*. New York: Simon & Schuster, 1956.

References

Zaleznik, Abraham. "Managers and leaders: Are they different?" *Harvard Business Review*, 1977, 55, p. 67–78.

Chapter Five

Abernathy, William J., Clark, Kim B., & Kantrow, Alan M. *Industrial Renaissance*. New York: Basic Books, 1983.

Burns, James MacGregor. *Leadership*. New York: Harper & Row, 1978. *Business Week*, February 13, 1984, pp. 98–100.

Commager, Henry Steele. *The American Mind*. New Haven: Yale University Press, 1950.

Drucker, Peter F. "Management's new role," *Harvard Business Review*, November–December 1969, pp. 49–54.

Gilder, George. *The Spirit of Enterprise*. New York: Simon & Schuster, 1984.

Gorer, Geoffrey. *The American People*. New York: Norton, 1964 (revised edition).

Hofstede, Geert. "Motivation, leadership and organization: Do American theories apply abroad?, *"Organizational Dynamics*, Summer 1980, pp. 42–63.

Hogan, Robert. "Theoretical egocentrism and the problem of compliance," *American Psychologist*, 1975, pp. 533–540.

McDermott, Kevin. "Loyal to what?," *SAM Advanced Management Review*, Spring 1982, 47, pp. 55–56.

Rickover, Hyman G. "Thoughts on the Presidency," *The New York Times*, February 21, 1982, pp. 1–19.

Schein, Edgar H. "SMR Forum: Does Japanese management style have a message for American managers?" *Sloan Management Review*, Fall 1981, pp. 55–68.

Silk, Leonard. "The painful shift to costly oil," *The New York Times*, September 28, 1983.

Thackray, John. "The new organization man," *Management Today*, September 1981, pp. 74–77, 168.

Tocqueville, Alexis de. *Democracy in America*, Vol. 1. New York: Knopf, 1963 (the Henry Reeve text, revised by Francis Bowen and later by Phillips Bradley).

Tocqueville, Alexis de. *Democracy in America*. New York: Mentor, 1956 (edited and abridged by Richard D. Heffner).

U.S., Congress, Senate, Committee on the Budget, *Consumer Confidence and Federal Economic Policy*, Washington, D.C.: U.S. Government Printing Office, 1975.

Chapter Six

Abernathy, William J., Clark, Kim B., & Kantrow, Alan M. *Industrial Renaissance*. New York: Basic Books, 1983.

Bryan, Leslie A., Jr. "The Japanese and the American first-line supervisor." *Training and Development Journal*, January 1982.

Cole, Robert E. "Learning from the Japanese: Prospects and pitfalls," *Management Review*, 1980, 69, pp. 9, 22–42.

Collison, Robert. "The Japanese Fix," *Canadian Business*, November 1981, pp. 37–48, 180.

Cristopher, Robert C. "Changing face of Japan," *The New York Times Magazine*, March 27, 1983, pp. 40–41, 81–83, 86–90, 100.

Fiske, Edward B. "Japan's schools: Not very much U.S. can borrow," *The New York Times*, July 13, 1983, p. A10.

Fukujiro, Sono. *Stages of growth*. Tokyo: TDK Electronics, 1980.

Golden, Arthur S. "Group think in Japan, Inc.," *The New York Times Magazine*, December 5, 1982, pp. 133–140.

Haberman, Clyde. "In Japan, a crime wave is measured in drops," *The New York Times*, August 2, 1983, p. A2.

Holusha, John. "Detroit's new labor strategy," *The New York Times*, Business Day, May 13, 1983, pp. 1, 3.

Hsu, F.L.K. *Iemoto: The Heart of Japan*. New York: Wiley, 1975.

Lim, Howard. "Japanese management: A skill profile, *Training and Development Journal*, October 1981, pp. 18–21.

Lohr, Steve. "Japan struggling with itself," *The New York Times*, Business Section, June 13, 1982, pp. 1, 6.

Lohr, Steve. "Matsushita: The cautious giant," *The New York Times*, Business Section, December 5, 1982, p. 4.

References

Lohr, Steve. "Overhauling America's business management," *The New York Times Magazine,* January 4, 1981, pp. 2–12.

Nippon Steel Corporation. *Nippon: The Land and Its People.* Japan: Gakuseisha, 1982.

Pascale, Richard T., & Athos, Anthony G. *The Art of Japanese Management.* New York: Warner, 1981.

Rehder, Robert R. "Japan's synergistic society," *Management Review,* 1981, 70, pp. 10, 64–66.

Salmans, Sandra. "American managers hear Japan's view," *The New York Times,* November 22, 1982, p. D1-D3.

Schein, Edgar H. "SMR Forum: Does Japanese management style have a message for American managers?" *Sloan Management Review,* Fall 1981, pp. 55–68.

"Where every worker is an inspector," *The Straits Times,* April 11, 1981, p. 8.

"Cooperation is the key to productivity," *The Straits Times,* April 10, 1981, p. 12.

Weisz, John R., Rothbaum, Fred M., & Blackburn, Thomas C. "Standing out and standing in: The psychology of control in America and Japan," *American Psychologist,* 1984, pp. 955–967.

Whitehall, A.M. "Cultural values and employee attitudes: United States and Japan," *Journal of Applied Psychology,* 1964, pp. 48, 68–72.

Yamamoto, Seiji. "Facts about Japanese industrial training," unpublished.

Yamamoto, Seiji. "Emerging trends of human resources management in Japan." Presented at the First International Conference on Human Resources Management, Manila, Philippines, 1982.

Chapter Seven

Bennis, Warren. "The five key traits of successful chief executives," *International Management,* October 1981, p. 60.

Blakely, Tom. "How to say 'no' to your boss," *Canadian Business,* September 1981, pp. 64–66.

Drucker, Peter F. *Adventures of a Bystander*. New York: Harper & Row, 1979.

Dunbar, Roger L.M., Dutton, John M., & Torbert, William R. "Crossing mother: Ideological constraints on organizational improvements," *Journal of Management Studies*, 1982, *19*, pp. 1, 91–108.

McIntyre, Shelby, H. "Obstacles to corporate innovation," *Business Horizons*, January–February 1982, pp. 23–28.

Moscovici, Serge, & Faucheux, Claude. Social influence, conformity bias, and the study of active minorities, in L. Berkowitz (Ed.) *Advances In Experimental Social Psychology*, Vol. 6., pp. 149–202. New York: Academic Press, 1972.

Peters, Thomas J., & Waterman, Robert H., Jr. *In Search of Excellence: Lessons from America's best run companies*. New York: Harper & Row, 1982.

Schilit, Warren K., & Locke, E.A. "A study of upward influence in organizations," *Administrative Science Quarterly*, 1982, *27*, pp. 304–316.

Wolf, Sharon. "Behavioral style and group cohesiveness as sources of minority influence," *European Journal of Social Psychology*, 1979, *9*, pp. 381–395.

Chapter Eight

Arbose, Jules, R. "Intrapreneurship: Holding on to people with ideas," *International Management*, March 1982, pp. 16–20.

Brown, Robert. "When a business matures: How to keep the entrepreneurial thrust," *Management Review*, 1980, *69*, pp. 4, 14–17.

Clutherbuck, David. "Blowing the whistle on corporate misconduct," *International Management*, 1980, *35*, pp. 1, 14–19.

Fowler, Elizabeth M. "Strategic corporate planners," *The New York Times*, Business Section, June 9, 1982, p. 3.

Fowler, Elizabeth M. "Managers to handle a crisis," *The New York Times*, January 30, 1985, p. D19.

References

French, James P. "Innovation breeds success," *Canadian Business,* October 1976, *49,* pp. 10, 42–46.

Harshbarger, Dwight. "The individual and the social order: Notes on the management of heresy and deviance in complex organizations," *Human Relations,* 1973, *26,* pp. 2, 251–269.

Hirschman, Albert O. *Exit, Voice and Loyalty.* Cambridge, MA: Harvard University Press, 1970.

Lawler, Edward E., & Drexler, John A. "Entrepreneurship in the corporation: Is it possible?," *Management Review,* 1981, *70,* pp. 2, 8–11.

Lohr, Steve. "Overhauling America's business management," *The New York Times Magazine,* January 4, 1981, pp. 2–12.

McAdams, Tony. "Speaking out in the corporate community," *Academy of Management Review,* 1977, *2,* pp. 2, 196–205.

McIntyre, Shelby, H. "Obstacles to corporate innovation," *Business Horizons,* January–February, 1982, pp. 23–28.

Moscovici, Serge, & Faucheux, Claude. "Social influence, conformity bias, and the study of active minorities," in L. Berkowitz (Ed.) *Advances In Experimental Social Psychology,* Vol. 6., pp. 149–202. New York: Academic Press, 1972.

"Organizing for innovation," *Insight* No. 410(10), Bureau of Business Practice, Waterford, CT, 1983.

Peters, Thomas J. *Hospital Forum,* May–June, 1982, pp. 2–5.

Peters, Thomas J., & Waterman, Robert H., Jr. *In Search of Excellence: Lessons from America's best run companies.* New York: Harper & Row, 1982.

Schein, Edgar H. SMR Forum: "Does Japanese management style have a message for American managers?" *Sloan Management Review,* Fall 1981, pp. 55–68.

Sloan, Alfred P. *My Years with General Motors.* Garden City, NY: Doubleday, 1964.

Taubman, Philip. "At State, dissent gives rise to praise," *The New York Times,* November 8, 1982, p. B-8

Thackray, John. "The new organization man," *Management Today,* September 1981, pp. 74–77, 168.

Tocqueville, Alexis de. *Democracy in America,* Vol. 1. New York: Knopf, 1963 (the Henry Reeve text, revised by Francis Bowen and later by Phillips Bradley).

Tocqueville, Alexis de. *Democracy in America.* New York: Mentor, 1956 (edited and abridged by Richard D. Heffner).

INDEX

Index

business issues, 133–134
challenging superiors, 133, 136
characteristics, 7
consequences of, 170–171
credibility and, 173–175
crime and, 165–166
decline in 1970s, 139–142
decline of after punishment, 74–80
direct action and, 176–178
disruptiveness of, 57–59
drama of, 31–32
on ethical principles, 133–134, 136
expertise and, 175
focus of, 171–173
guidelines for, 171–185
harmony stifles, 22, 103–104
history of, 25–26
impact of economy, 139
importance of, 3–5
indirect action and, 176–178
industry differences on, 68–69
in Japan, 155–160
leadership and, 107–108
limits of, 188–190
management education and, 114
management styles and, 139–140
managers' opinion of, 2–3, 68–69
motives for, 41–42
in new generation, 140–141
vs. obedience, 98
occurrence of, 69
organization response to, 72–80
for painful problems, 182–185
patience and persistence, 178–182
risk of, 29–30
role of predictability, 175
stifled by egalitarianism, 102–103
subordinates' support, 91–93
success and failure compared in
    Japan and U.S., 155–160
success linked to manager's position,
    93–98
success rate in Japan, 164–165
success rate in U.S., 132
superiors' support, 91–92
supporters' characteristics, 92–93

supporters vs. saboteurs, 178–182
timing of, 182–185
towards subordinates, 133
years of occurrence, 128, 134–135
Courageous managers:
defined, 34
interviews with, 35–44
motivation, 36
summarized, 43–44
Cowardice:
in conforming managers, 59
in silenced managers, 59–62
Credibility, courageous behavior and,
    173–175
Crime, courageous behavior and,
    165–166
Crisis:
courage and, 115
managerial behavior during,
    135–136
Cultural differences, American and
    Japanese, 24
Culturally induced dispositions, 152
Cyert, Richard, 14

Dana Corporation, 198–199
de Cervantes, Miguel, 184–185
De Tocqueville, Alexis:
on continuity-discontinuity tension,
    203
on popular mandate philosophy,
    119–120
on tyranny of majority, 99–100
Decentralization of management, 90
Decision-making in Japanese business,
    153–155, 161–162
Dematurity of industry, 14
Desperation, courageous behavior and,
    42
Direct action:
consequences in Japan, 177
courageous behavior and, 176–178
Disaffected managers:
behavior of, 52–55
defined, 34
Disclaimers of self-identity, 39

Index

Index

Index

DATE DUE
